Praise for *The STOP Program for Women Who Abuse*

"David Wexler understands the importance of developing scientifically proven and accessible programs aimed at a specific population. . . . [A] very useful manual for programs providing education on domestic violence, anger management, abuse, and sexual violence. . . . [A] wonderful first step in teaching clients how to have healthy engagement within their relationships."

—**PsychCentral**

"Finally! We have needed a program for recognizing and helping with female domestic violence for decades. Just talking about it is an immense contribution. A clinically sensitive and thorough intervention is a miracle. David Wexler has made an enormous contribution. This book is a must-read!"

—**John Gottman,** author of *The Seven Principles for Making Marriage Work*

"Once again, David Wexler has offered a practical, comprehensive, gender-sensitive handbook on how to treat individuals who are aggressive and abusive—now with evidence-based interventions for the long-overlooked population of women who abuse. This group leader's manual and the accompanying handouts and homework will be of great value to all clinicians. Kudos to David Wexler!"

—**Donald Meichenbaum, PhD,** Distinguished Professor Emeritus, University of Waterloo, and research director of the Melissa Institute for Violence Prevention

"David Wexler brings his considerable experience and expertise to the treatment of abusive, violent women in this straightforward and user-friendly manual. It will be invaluable not only for the beginning practitioner but also informative to the seasoned facilitator of groups for women. Highly recommended."

—**Ellen L. Bowen,** LCSW, BCD, cofounder of NOVA Non-Violent Alternatives, and author of *Domestic Violence Treatment for Abusive Women—A Treatment Manual*

"With Wexler's comprehensive intervention approach, a previously poorly understood population is now given new hope through understanding the reasons, reactions, and responses to female aggression and its etiology—paving the way for effective treatment. This step-by-step manual will guide new or seasoned professionals alike in aiding the recovery of a new frontier of IPV population. Well done!"

—**Sandra L. Brown,** MA, The Institute for Relational Harm Reduction & Public Pathology Education

The STOP Program for Women Who Abuse

The STOP Program for Women Who Abuse

GROUP LEADER'S MANUAL

SECOND EDITION

David B. Wexler

Norton Professional Books

An Imprint of W. W. Norton & Company
Independent Publishers Since 1923

For information about special discounts for bulk purchases, please contact W. W. Norton Special Sales at specialsales@wwnorton.com or 800-233-4830

Manufacturing by Versa Press
Production manager: Gwen Cullen

ISBN: 978-1-324-05385-9 (pbk)

W. W. Norton & Company, Inc., 500 Fifth Avenue, New York, NY 10110
www.wwnorton.com

W. W. Norton & Company Ltd., 15 Carlisle Street, London W1D 3BS

1 2 3 4 5 6 7 8 9 0

To all the women who are courageous enough to change their lives

Contents

Acknowledgments

The original development of *The STOP Program* treatment model for domestic violence emerged from a collaborative effort as part of a research project evaluating military domestic violence treatment programs, cosponsored by the Department of Defense and the National Institute of Mental Health. The research was conducted by a team from the University of Colorado, headed by principal investigator Franklyn W. Dunford, PhD, who offered sage counsel and impeccable support to the fine-tuning of this program. I would like to particularly express my gratitude to the US Navy Family Advocacy Program administrators and staff for offering so much support and invaluable creative contributions to this body of work throughout the years.

The San Diego Domestic Violence Council, and the coordinated community efforts of city attorney Casey Gwinn, the district attorney, the police department, the judges, the community agencies, and the victim support groups, have provided an extremely fertile climate for the development of these ideas.

Many thanks also to my mentors and heroes in this sacred work: Donald Dutton, John Gottman, Amy Holtzworth-Munroe, Sue Johnson, Jackson Katz, Ron Levant, Don Meichenbaum, Bill O'Hanlon, Bill Pollack, and Terry Real. And also thanks to those who have guided our work in helping understand women who abuse and for the unique challenges of helping women grow and change: Julia Babcock, Ellen Bowen, Robert Geffner, John Hamel, Michele Koonin, Lisa Larance, and Suzanne Swan.

Finally, thanks to all the women and men who have given so much of themselves and worked so hard throughout our years of treatment. We have found that people who commit acts of domestic violence come in many shapes and sizes and genders and sexual orientations—and that each of them has a unique story to tell.

Introduction to the Second Edition

Six decades ago, intimate partner violence was barely recognized. Two decades later, men's abuse of women had come fully out of the shadows. Not until three decades ago did those of us in this field begin to recognize that female intimate partner violence (of their male partners or in same-sex relationships) actually might be a legitimate phenomenon that was not simply a reaction to ongoing male abuse. But still, when we trained mental health professionals, probation officers, victims' programs, attorneys, and correctional officers all over the world, we had to convince people there was such a thing as female domestic violence. Two decades ago, we began to recognize that there really was a significant pattern of bidirectional abuse in many relationships (once we got rid of the label of "mutually violent abuse"). And around that same time, we began to more fully develop domestic violence treatment programs for female offenders and pursue research on the typologies of female offenders.

In 2016—based on the decades of developments in understanding and treating female abuse—we published *The STOP Program for Women Who Abuse.* Hundreds of agencies have adopted this model, and thousands of female offenders have completed the program.

Now, with the help of valuable feedback from agencies and group facilitators—and with more and more research clarifying the central dynamics at play—we present a new and improved version: *The STOP Program for Women Who Abuse, Second Edition.*

This upgraded treatment focuses on an increased emphasis on both trauma theory and attachment theory, new material based on research on criminogenic thinking patterns, and an increased emphasis on both mindfulness techniques and gratitudes (based on contemporary research). Also included are new field-tested sessions on the Five Love Languages, the Adverse Childhood Experiences (ACE) Study, the Stages of Change, and Stake in Conformity.

Furthermore, we have tried to redesign the program material to be user-friendly for same-sex or bisexual offenders (and even transgender offenders who identify as female). Historically, straight and gay offenders have been treated separately in both the men's and women's groups. However, in recent years many programs have experimented with integrating heterosexual and same-sex or bisexual offenders (and transgender offenders who identify as female) in the same group—with very promising results. Some of the focus on male-female gender roles may not apply, but the central themes of *The STOP Program for Women Who Abuse*, Second Edition (and the experience of being female) definitely do.

Please note that many of the examples and vignettes in this new manual now use the term *partner* and alternately refer to one's partner as *him* or *her*, to make this more user-friendly to both straight and LGBTQ+ group members.

Finally, because the use of carefully selected video clips is so essential to the unique success of this program, the new manual incorporates several new videos throughout the sessions.

NOTE: *The STOP Program for Women, Second Edition: Handouts and Homework* is the companion piece for group members. Fully integrated with *The STOP Program for Women Who Abuse, Second Edition: Group Leader's Manual*, these handouts are critical to keeping group members actively engaged in overcoming their abusive behaviors. Packaged as functional loose-leaf sheets, they can be added, removed, or rearranged to suit the needs of any group leader. Each participant receives her own set of *Handouts and Homework* and brings this with her to each group session.

PLEASE NOTE: ALL GROUP MEMBERS MUST HAVE THEIR OWN PERSONAL ORIGINAL COPY OF *Homework and Handouts*—COPYING THESE FORMS IS A VIOLATION OF COPYRIGHT LAWS. Exceptions are made for the Weekly Check-In Form and Evaluation Form.

Introduction to the First Edition

It used to be that, when we trained mental health professionals, probation officers, victims' program staff, attorneys, and correctional officers all over the world, we had to convince people there was such a thing as female domestic violence.

But over the past decade, the landscape has shifted—and instead we hear pleas everywhere for a quality treatment program for women who abuse that is specifically targeted to women's issues.

So, after years of pilot group testing, integrating rapidly emerging new research trends, and borrowing from the tremendous success of *The STOP Program for Men* (now in its third edition, published in 2013), this new treatment program was hatched: *The STOP Program for Women,* focusing on innovative strategies for women who abuse their partners.

Like the men's manual, this new program integrates contemporary interventions and client-centered guidelines to successfully treat domestic violence offenders—who happen to be female.

This program is timed to address the rapidly increasing awareness of female domestic violence and the need for quality treatment services. Developed and field tested for over 25 years among military and civilian populations internationally, this program offers therapists, social workers, and other counselors a new level of sound, psychologically based interventions that actually reach the very women who often seem so unapproachable in a treatment setting.

Presented in a 26-week or 52-week psychoeducational format, *The STOP Program for Women* is packed with updated skills, training exercises, articles, video clips, handouts, homework, and other resources that push participants to examine the complex roles of trauma, emotional dysregulation, self-esteem deficits, and histories of personal victimization in their relationship problems. And the program gives them new tools to manage these unique issues.

This manual includes many of the same sessions as the original *STOP Program* for men, with appropriate changes in pronouns, vignettes, and examples. We also have developed and integrated new material specifically dealing with issues that contemporary research and our clinical experience indicate are especially relevant for female offenders: victimization (and rationalization) issues, assertiveness versus aggression issues, shame, grief and loss, parenting and coparenting, boundary violations, emotional self-management and dysregulation issues, jealousy, self-esteem issues, gender rules and gender roles, and need for social support.

Finally (based on innovative new trends in treating substance abuse issues concurrently with domestic violence) we are including guidelines for every session for a substance abuse focus on female domestic violence treatment. This option will be invaluable to programs that need to address these co-occurring issues together.

The STOP Program for Women: Handouts and Homework is the companion piece for group members. Fully integrated with *The STOP Program for Women: Group Leader's Manual*, these handouts are critical to keeping group members actively engaged in overcoming their abusive behaviors. Packaged as functional loose-leaf sheets, they can be added, removed, or rearranged to suit the needs of any group leader. Each participant receives her own set of *Handouts and Homework* and brings this with her to each group session.

PLEASE NOTE: ALL GROUP MEMBERS MUST HAVE THEIR OWN PERSONAL ORIGINAL COPY OF *Homework and Handouts*— COPYING THESE FORMS IS A VIOLATION OF COPYRIGHT LAWS.

The STOP Program for Women Who Abuse

PART I

FOUNDATIONS AND GUIDELINES

WHAT WE NOW KNOW ABOUT FEMALE INTIMATE PARTNER VIOLENCE:

SPECIAL ISSUES

We all carry many preconceptions that either downplay female violence and highlight male violence—or that don't take into account the genuine ways in which female intimate partner violence (IPV) often needs to be understood in the context of the male violence in these women's lives.

The story that we generate in understanding female IPV can either lead us astray or help us focus on the central issues at hand.

Pay attention to which of the following two statements you feel most aligned with:

- *Female intimate partner violence is essentially the same as male intimate partner violence, and should be treated the same way.*

If you are more likely to think along these lines, then you run the risk of ignoring the profound role that "coercive control" plays in many male-to-female abusive relationships—a role that is noticeably absent the other way around. You also may minimize the extremely prevalent history of female trauma in previous relationships as well as her current one. And you might miss out on designing female IPV treatment groups that focus on issues like reactivity to emotional abuse, self-defense and fear issues, fears of abandonment, and PTSD reactions.

- *Women can't really be perpetrators of intimate partner violence—this always needs to be understood in the context of self-defense.*

If you believe this, then you might make the mistake of allowing female IPV treatment groups to degenerate into sessions focused primarily on victim-hood. You may discount men's reports of abuse from women. And you might unintentionally contribute to the disempowerment of women by identifying them as incapable of independent behavior.

One classic study (Follingstad, 2004) highlights the ways in which female IPV is often minimized. This research was actually based on responses from psychologists—who you think would know better. They were given vignettes in which one person was insisting that his or her partner had to account for their whereabouts at all times, weren't allowed to look at members of the opposite sex, suffered through derogatory comments, and were threatened with being institutionalized for being "crazy." When the vignette was presented with the male as the abusive partner, the psychologists rated the situation as much more abusive and dangerous. When the perpetrator of these abusive behaviors was described as being female, the dangerous and abusive ratings were much lower.

It is incumbent on those of us working in the field to confront our biases and respond to what is actually taking place in front of us. And the truth, as always, lies somewhere in between the different stories above—and the same can be said about many other stories that show the complexity of relationship violence.

Does Female-to-Male Intimate Partner Violence Really Exist?

Female IPV in straight relationships actually exists—not *just* in self-defense and not *just* as retaliation for longstanding abuse by a male partner, but where the primary source of the violence is actually from the woman. That represents a smaller percentage of overall IPV, compared to violence initiated and implemented by men, but we now know that it really does exist.

In fact, the trend throughout intimate partner violence research tells us that there is a higher frequency of female-to-male IPV than we previously believed. When physical aggression is the subject of inquiry (as opposed to sexual coercion, psychological abuse, coercive control, or stalking)—despite the fact that criminal databases estimate that about nine times as many men as women perpetrate violence (in other words, about one of every ten IPV arrests is female)—we know from multiple incidence studies (not criminal records) that the actual frequency of women initiating abusive behavior is about equal to men.

Family violence surveys, such as the National Family Violence Survey (Stets, 1990), consistently find that women initiate mild-to-moderate physical assaults towards their male partners with about the same frequency as men. In fact, this finding has been replicated in over 100 studies (Straus, 1999). Women are only *sometimes* motivated by self-defense, which contradicts what we used to believe, and bidirectional violence is actually the most common subcategory of IPV (Swan, 2005; Johnson, 2008).

But not in all categories. Yes, in *situational couple violence,* or *SCV* (Johnson, 2008), studies indicate that women and men are equally likely to initiate. In contrast, in the more serious and more likely to be extremely violent *intimate terrorism,* or *IT* (characterized by the most pathological and destructive patterns of coercive control in relationships), men are much, much more likely to be perpetrators. In fact, among the relationships identified as characterized by *intimate terrorism*, Johnson's (2008; 2000) studies indicate that as many of 97% of the IPV perpetrators are male.

What is Different About Women's Abuse of Intimate Partners?

In many ways, perhaps the most important ways, all intimate partner violence is alike: male, female, gay, straight, Latino, Black, upper middle class, and lower class, research indicates that female IPV offenders share many of the same characteristics as male offenders, including similar motives and demographics, like prior history of aggression, substance use, personality disturbance, etc. (Carney, 2007). Male and female IPV offenders share many familial risk factors (more similarities than differences) for intimate abuse, like witnessing interparental abuse, receiving physical abuse by a caregiver, substance abuse, etc.

In a classic study by Swan (2002), female IPV offenders reported committing substantial levels of abusive behavior. Almost all of the women committed moderate physical violence; 57% committed severe violence, 54% injured their partners, 28% (surprisingly!) used sexual coercion, and 86% used some form of coercive control.

However, while multiple survey studies (Straus, 1999) find that women and men perpetrate roughly equivalent levels of mild-to-moderate physical and psychological aggression, we also find that women are also much more frequently injured during IPV incidents (Archer, 2000; Sorenson, 1996). Women are also much more likely to require medical attention for their injuries (Tjaden, 2000), to take time off from work (Stets, 1990; Tjaden, 2000), and to use mental health and criminal justice system services (Tjaden, 2000).

Furthermore, although women committed equivalent levels of emotional abuse and moderate physical abuse as compared to their male partners, they reported that their male partners committed significantly more of the following classic battering behaviors: sexual coercion, injury, and severe physical violence.

Many other studies confirm that men perpetrate more sexual coercion (Archer, 2000; Katz, 2002; Menard, 2003; O'Sullivan, 2001; Straus, 1996; Struckman-Johnson, 2003; West, 2000). And when it comes to stalking, The National Violence Against Women Survey (a nationally representative survey of 8,000 men and 8,000 women in the United States), found the lifetime prevalence of having experienced stalking was 14.2% for women and 4.3% for men (Davis 2002). Women were 13 times as likely as men to report being very afraid of the stalker (Davis, 2002).

Most importantly, while in many ways, more and more studies indicate similarities between female-to-male IPV compared to the other way round, there is one very important component that is almost exclusively found male-to-female: the use of "coercive control." Although women and men are equally likely to initiate violence in less serious "situational couple violence" relationships, in the most serious and very violent *intimate terrorism* relationships, men are very much more likely to be perpetrators, and women victims.

Coercive control is not just psychological aggression (which both genders are quite capable of inflicting). Coercive control was originally represented in the *Power & Control Wheel* developed by the Duluth programs for IPV (Pence, 1993) and has been further delineated by Johnson in his work distinguishing IPV typologies (Johnson, 2008). This is a pattern of nonphysical (and some physical) tactics used by abusers to maintain control over their partners, including intimidation, isolation, economic control, controlling partner's activities and decisions, emotional abuse, erosion of independence, and self-esteem. Stark (2006) makes a strong argument that the coercive control pattern, more than physical aggression alone, is central to the powerful and dangerous effects.

And this pattern of pervasive coercive control, in conjunction with physical aggression, is an almost exclusively male phenomenon.

Motivations: Why Do Women Do It?

Also, in making sense of female IPV towards men, it is crucial to examine the issue of female motivation for violence. Remember the basic hypothesis that most of us in the field *used to* subscribe to: Violence towards men by women must always be understood in a context of self-defense, either obvious legal self-defense, like "He's drunk and he's coming after me to attack me and I pick up a knife" that even the law would recognize as self-defense. Or, in the case of a broader definition of self-defense (often referred to in forensic settings as *imperfect self-defense*); "I've been beaten down by him so many times I just had to do something to stave off more beating." Or so we thought.

Clearly—especially among men who engage in *intimate terrorism*—the cases of IPV involve many men who are motivated primarily by needs for power and control, and many more women than men who are motivated by a need (or at least a perceived need) for self-defense and protection (Barnett, 1997; Swan, 2006).

However, in a study examining men and women's motives for perpetrating violence in dating relationships, Harned (2001) found that men and women actually were *equally likely* to report perpetrating IPV in self-defense. (Of course this would not apply to cases of *intimate terrorism*.) In fact, study after study (Hamberger, 1994; Follingstad, 1991; Straus, 1992; Fiebert, 1997; Hettrich, 2007; Foshee, 2001; Cascardi, 1995; Harned, 2001; Weston, 2007; Barnett, 1997) tell us that only a minority of women who are violent with their male partners attributed their aggression primarily to self-defense. Although many women may use the language of "self defense," closer examination identifies descriptions that are more consistent with *retaliation* and *retribution* (Carrado, 1996; Harned, 2001).

Across these different studies, in response to the question of "Why did you assault your partner?" or "What is the function, purpose, or payoff of your violence?", the primary responses were as follows:

- **To express feelings** (*I wanted him to know how upset I was.*)
- **To enforce an ethic** (*He cheated on me* or *He treated me badly in some way. He's not going to get away with that crap and this is my way of letting him know.*)
- **Retaliation** for previous harm or emotional abuse (*I just wanted him to shut up. He was criticizing me and talking to me and I threw this thing at him or I kicked him or whatever I did.*)
- **To engage his attention** (*He wouldn't talk to me. How else was I supposed to let him know? He has to talk to me.*)
- **To gain control** or assert authority: One study (Swan, 2003) found that 38% of female IPV offenders stated that they had threatened to use violence at least sometimes to make their partner do the things they wanted him to do.
- **Self-defense, protection, or fear** (Some studies indicate that this was absolutely the primary motivation for some women, while many others identify this only in a minority of cases.)

We also know that both women and men use violence in retribution for their partners' attacks against them (Hamberger, 1997). However, men are somewhat more likely to use violence in retribution for their partners' unwanted behavior, such as infidelity or lying, while women are more likely to be motivated by retribution for the partners' emotionally abusive behavior (e.g., "punishment for his insults").

What is particularly striking about these findings is how comparable these motivations are for men (at least the men who engage in *situational couple violence* rather than *intimate terrorism*). The predominant motivations from male offenders (again, with the very notable exception of men in the *intimate terrorism* category) involve very similar explanations as from female offenders: "to express my feelings," "to enforce an ethic," "to get her attention," etc. All of those motivations are painfully human, and they cross genders. The list of motivations above is not an exclusively female list.

However, even though research is informing us that much female IPV is attributable to other motivations besides self-defense, we can't ignore the obvious: There are still plenty of women who are identified as violent who were actually responding in self-defense. Studies of domestically violent women consistently find that the majority have also experienced violence from their male partners. Although these numbers vary across many studies, the nationally representative National Family Violence Survey reports that 64% of the women who used violence also experienced violence from their male partners (Stets, 1990). For many domestically violent women, their violence needs to be understood within the context of victimization from their male partners.

Some of the most pathological male batterers have mastered the art of inflicting physical damage without leaving visible bruises or injury, and some of their partners do leave marks and injuries on the men when fighting back. I treated one case where the man had pinned his wife down, yanked her by the hair, and crushed her to the point where she passed out. She was able to struggle and pick up a knife and chase him out of the house—which was when the police arrived her and saw her with a weapon and him running away. *She* was arrested.

Origins of Female IPV

We are now finding out more and more about the psychological factors that predict, or at least correlate with, female IPV. Compared to non-offending females, female IPV offenders show evidence of significantly more trauma-related symptoms, greater attachment insecurity (fears of abandonment, poorer emotional regulation, jealousy), and more Axis II/Cluster-B personality disorders (antisocial, borderline, histrionic, and narcissistic traits) (Goldenson, 2007).

TRAUMA HISTORY

Evidence from several different studies indicates that rates of childhood trauma and abuse are very high among women who use violence. Swan's study (2003) found that 35% of female IPV offenders reported experiencing childhood physical abuse, 37% emotional abuse, and 35% sexual abuse. In multiple other studies of women in court-mandated IPV treatment, similarly high rates of childhood victimization have been found (Hamberger, 1994; Leisring, 2003).

Many of these women have missed out on key components of positive family life because of parental abandonment, mental illness, or substance abuse. Furthermore, most have been on the receiving end of physical or sexual abuse in teen or adult romantic relationships—and many of them have also been on the receiving end of abuse with their current partners. Anyone with his kind of history is highly likely to have impaired coping skills and emotional self-regulations skills, particularly emerging in their most intimate relationships.

ATTACHMENT DISORDERS

Carney (2007) found that women identified as being highly dependent on their partners—an adult indicator of *preoccupied attachment* style—showed much higher levels of perpetrating psychological aggression, physical assault, and injury. Margolies (1995) found that these women were overly dependent on attention and close involvement of their partners and were unable to convey their emotional needs clearly.

PSYCHOLOGICAL FUNCTIONING/EMOTIONAL SELF-REGULATION

Swan (2003) found that 60% of the women who had used violence against an intimate partner in their sample met clinical criteria for depression. Henning (2003) compared the psychological functioning of men and women arrested for IPV and found that women were even more likely than men to score in the clinical range for major depression and bipolar disorder, among others.

Furthermore, the inability to regulate emotions is associated with an increased likelihood of perpetrating partner violence (McNulty, 2008; Shorey, 2011). In fact, female IPV offenders were even more likely than male IPV offenders to show traits of Axis II/Cluster B personality disorders (Simmons, 2005; Varley Thornton, 2010). The authors conclude that these women might be more likely to perpetrate IPV when they are angry or when their needs are not met, which is consistent with theories that individuals engage in partner violence to regulate negative emotional states, such as anger. Furthermore, female IPV offenders were found to have particular tendencies towards black and white thinking (Margolies, 1995).

TYPOLOGIES OF FEMALE IPV OFFENDERS

Just as we have seen from several decades of research on male IPV offenders, we now are seeing at least the beginning of clarification about the different types of female IPV offenders. Although this research is still in the early stages, the field has generated some insight into the personality characteristics and background risk factors for women who abuse their partners. Integrating the findings from multiple different clinicians and other researchers (Bowen, 2008; Conradi et al., 2009; Henning & Holdford, 2006; Swan & Snow, 2003) leads us to identify the following four types of FIPV offenders.

PRIMARY AGGRESSORS *(Women who initiate unprovoked aggressive reactions)*

These women often use force based on a sense of entitlement and control (often as a result of lifetime victimization, trauma, and subjugation). Many of these women share the traditional criminogenic beliefs that we typically see in aggressive men (violence is normal, beat or be beaten, I just get out of control, etc.).

VIOLENT REACTIVE OR VIOLENT RETALIATION *(Women [whose current partners have a long-standing history of controlling and abusing them] who respond violently—but not specifically in self-defense)*

This woman has at least some episodes of violence but doesn't engage in coercive control, but her male partner is both violent and controlling and much more frequently the primary aggressor.

Think of the story popularized in the 1984 movie *The Burning Bed*, where a woman burns down the house with her husband in it after years of his relentless abuse. She believes she has no other means of escape from being killed by him.

Some of the common triggers for this type of FIPV are the following:

- Impulsive Reaction: An instinctive reaction to being attacked, and it happens at the first blow—almost without thought.
- Justice and Retaliation: *What you're doing isn't right and I'm going to fight back as hard as I can.*
- Escape: Fearing that the assaults will continue forever if something isn't done to stop them. For a few, eventually it seems that the only way out is to kill their partner.

In understanding this type of FIPV, it should be noted that 51% of females who kill their partners (but only 14% of males who kill theirs) had been physically abused by the victim prior to the lethal incident (Yourstone et al., 2008). Self-defense played a role in 36% of the cases involving a female killer, compared with only 1% of male-perpetrated homicides of the female partner (Weizmann-Henelius et al., 2011).

BIDIRECTIONAL *(Women who are in bidirectional aggressive relationships)*

This used to be identified as mutually violent aggression or mutual combat, but bidirectional is the more contemporary term. Couples report relatively low levels of victimization (56%; damage and impact equivalent for males and females). In a review of 50 studies, 57.9% of IPV was bidirectional, where both reported at least some abuse.

By itself, this is not a particularly meaningful finding, because there are many abusive heterosexual relationships in which one person (usually the male) is predominantly aggressive, and the other person (usually the female) is only occasionally aggressive. To help us make this label of bidirectional abuse relevant, a classic study (Vivian & Langhinrichsen-Rohling, 1994) found that 56% of the couples in which both partners had at least sometimes been aggressive reported low to moderate levels of aggression—with physical and psychological damage and impact equivalent for males and females. That is a good description of bidirectional abuse. And it suggests that (inexact as these categories and criteria are) approximately 32% (56% of the 57.9% figure above) can actually be conceptualized and treated as bidirectional abuse. For many people, this is a new concept. But for most people who actually work in the trenches treating individuals and couples with issues of IPV, it actually confirms what our eyes and ears have been telling us for many years.

SELF-DEFENSE *(Women acting in direct self-defense, according to the definition provided by legal statutes)*

The courts have defined the term imminent danger as meaning "peril must have existed or appeared to the defendant to have existed at the very time the fatal shot was fired. . . . Peril must appear to the defendant as immediate and present and not prospective or even in the near future . . . must be instantly dealt with" (Judicial Council of California Advisory Committee, 2014, p. 26).

One caveat: In some cases, women may be perpetrating as much or more physical violence than their partners, but their partners may be committing other types of abuse that are not always considered, such as sexual abuse or coercive control.

How Are Women Affected Differently from Men?

Studies of couples in mutually violent relationships find more negative effects for women in these relationships than for men.

Furthermore, women are injured more than men and women are killed more than men (Carney, 2007). And, very significantly, women are *intimidated* by abusive behavior from their partners much more than men.

Although few studies comparing gender differences of the effects of IPV have been conducted, the studies that have examined mutually violent couples suggest that women suffer more ill effects than men in such relationships. Anderson (2002) examined 474 couples reporting mutual violence and found that being in a mutually violent relationship predicted greater depression among both men and women—but, the effect was approximately twice as great for women.

A similar pattern was observed for drug and alcohol problems. While being in a relationship involving mutual violence predicted greater drug and alcohol problems among both men and women, the effect was greater for women. In a study of bidirectional violent couples receiving marital therapy, women reported feeling more sad, angry, frustrated, anxious, and afraid in response to their marital conflicts as compared to their husbands (Langhinrichsen-Rohling, 1995). And a study with a college sample found that partner violence generated more severe losses in relationship satisfaction for women as compared to men (Katz, 2002).

CLINICAL AND GROUP GUIDELINES

Our philosophy about IPV groups is that all IPV is the same: black, white, male, female, gay, straight, etc.—except when it's not. In other words, there are certain core elements about the triggers and dynamics of IPV that are shared among every group, regardless of the particular subtype we're talking about. In all programs and with all different subcategories of offenders, we insist on 100% responsibility; we focus on the ways people lie to each other and betray each other; we identify ways that partners show each other disrespect; we emphasize the dysfunctional patterns generated from attachment issues and personality disorders; and—when appropriate—we help offenders recognize power and control dynamics in abusive relationships.

But, even with these overarching similarities, different segments of our society are clearly, well, different. African American men are often dealing with issues of disempowerment. Gays and lesbians often fear police disrespect or aggression. And female IPV offenders are typically dealing with long histories of victimization—sexual, physical, and emotional—that contribute to the emergence of their own intimate partner violence.

Just as we have learned over decades with male IPV offenders, one size does not fit all for FIPV offenders. We know that many of these women have been victimized and traumatized by men in their lives—but treating all women arrested for FIPV as victims first and offenders second may miss important aspects of our mission. We need to differentiate between women who need victim services, women who need offender treatment, and women who need a combination of the two.

THE ISSUES IN THE ROOM

In our group treatment of FIPV offenders, the women in the room may all have arrived at violent behavior in their relationships for widely different reasons, such as:

- Breakdowns in emotional self-regulation
- Chronic passivity that erupts into aggression
- Attachment disorder (preoccupied/anxious)
- Attachment disorder (dismissing/avoidant)
- History of victimization by men
- Long-standing criminogenic beliefs or antisocial attitudes
- Violent reactive retaliation
- Dysfunctional bidirectional relationship

And, of course, many of them have multiple factors from this list.

The STOP Program for Women Who Abuse takes these factors carefully into account. It has become clear that programs treating female IPV offenders should retain much of what and how we traditionally treat men—but it is not sufficient to just take a men's group curriculum, change the gender pronouns, and administer it to women. It is certainly not relevant to emphasize power and control dynamics in relationships when treating female IPV offenders, because this is so rarely the motivation or the best narrative for female abusive behavior.

The curriculum should (and *The STOP Program for Women Who Abuse* does) include more emphasis on the following issues and themes:

- Trauma issues, because such a high percentage of female offenders have experienced trauma and are suffering from some form of PTSD
- Emotional self-regulation and behavioral options in a crisis (because so many female IPV offenders are in very stormy and volatile relationships)
- The tendency for many female IPV offenders to minimize their responsibility for their own actions because they feel emotionally justified or previously victimized
- Self-esteem and empowerment issues—and how to be an empowered female without resorting to aggression or emotional abuse
- The roles and expectations in relationships and how to establish self-protective and respectful boundaries

Group Process and Group Structure

Our decades of experience in treatment of female IPV offenders have generated valuable guidelines for offering the most relevant and successful interventions (thanks to Karen Z. Hyland, PhD, for many of these clinical observations). Female IPV offenders usually push much more for process in these groups (talking about group dynamics and relationships), whereas the men usually prefer to talk about skills and treat it more like a class. The women in the groups (big surprise!) want to talk more about their feelings, want to talk more about the feelings within their relationships, want to talk about their group experience and how they felt when so-and-so cut them off last week in the group session. The men in our programs usually don't talk like that. I'm not saying they never do, but they do not focus on their feelings and relationship process to the degree that women in these groups do.

Again, it is dangerous and unproductive to make extreme generalizations about how all women's groups are different from all men's groups. However, the following patterns typically show up in greater frequency and intensity in female IPV offenders' groups.

In general:

- The women are much more vocal and require more frequent therapist containment to keep the group on track.
- The women have more difficulty with group therapist turnover and need to process these changes more extensively (we often make sure that, whenever possible, the group members get at least six weeks' heads-up about a staff change so they can process the loss).
- Furthermore, the adjustment period when new members enter the group is usually more complex and of longer duration than in men's groups.
- The women's groups are more likely to spark emotional volatility than the men's groups—the mean levels of emotional fragility are usually higher (often including elements of borderline personality organization), and this can sometimes generate higher levels of conflict and vindictiveness within the women's groups.

- Anger is more directly focused on group leaders (*I'm not getting anything out of this; you're not like the last therapist; this lesson is useless; we need to talk*, etc.).
- Compared to men, the women in these groups tend to offer a lot more support outside the group (phone numbers, texting, sharing child care, etc.).
- Discussion about parenting issues is usually much more frequent.
- These groups typically have much more open and detailed discussions about sex, emotional intimacy, family dynamics from childhood, child raising, and trauma stories than male groups.

Assertiveness and Finding Her Voice

One of the most crucial challenges in FIPV groups is helping women find a voice to express their thoughts, needs, feelings, and opinions—in a way that is unlikely to generate defensiveness or aggression in her partner.

Not only is this simply good relationship behavior—it is also quite pragmatic. Research (Murphy & O'Leary, 1989) and common sense tell us that psychologically abusive behavior precedes and predicts the development of physically abusive behavior in relationships—therefore, reducing psychological aggression in both partners is likely to reduce IPV.

There is often a lot of resistance to this in the female groups, as many women have trouble grasping how their verbal and psychological aggression toward their partner actually puts them at greater risk. Selling the notion of approaching their partners in more respectful ways is often complicated by their belief that this is weak or passive. The group needs to relentlessly reframe assertive communicating as an expression of strength and not weakness.

One specific pitfall to be aware of is the actual implementation of so-called assertive communication skills. We often hear a woman coming back into the group reporting proudly that she "got assertive" with him—by yelling, screaming, and humiliating him. We then go back to the drawing board by pointing out that this was not assertive behavior—this was actually yelling, screaming, humiliating, abusive behavior instead.

Our groups also emphasize the value of choosing the right time and language for confrontation, conflict, or discussion. Choosing wisely is not submissive, compliant, or weak but simply respectful and good judgment.

One further note: Actual implementation of mature and successful assertive communication skills is impossible without developing some core skills in emotional self-regulation. None of us can moderate our language, tone, and timing when we are emotionally flooded. So the skills component of self-regulation and identifying signs of escalation has to be solidly in place for the fruits of the assertiveness components to have a positive impact.

Anger and Responsibility

Another clinical challenge is that women are less likely to view their aggression as violence. In fact, both men and women tend not to view women's aggressive acts as assaults—men do not identify with the label of *victim* and women do not identify with the label of *perpetrator*. The vast majority of women in our groups readily admit aggressive behavior but view it as justified because of the bad behavior of their partner—feeling even more justified than many men do.

When talking with female offenders, it's probably wisest to use language like "physical conflict" or "physical altercation" or "the time when you scratched his face" rather than asking about their violence or assaults or abuse. It is not worth it to generate any more resistance, denial, and defensiveness than we have to—as long as the women are able to face what actually happened with increased consciousness and with what needs to happen differently in the future.

We also notice a frequent pattern of female IPV offenders not taking responsibility because of the experience of having no self-control:

- *I just get angry, and there's nothing I can do about it.*
- *It just came over me, and I couldn't stop myself.*
- *Feelings are feelings, and I'm somebody who has to be real.*

They also often turn to the other group members and the group leaders to fix their problems—and become angry and blaming when the group hasn't "done its job."

Victimization and Accountability: When Women Feel Entitled

Often, women rationalize their abusive and/or violent behavior toward their partners because they have experienced themselves as victims and now feel entitled to retaliate. This is one of the most important issues in the treatment of FIPV offenders, and it often shows up when women feel emotionally injured or betrayed.

I evaluated one female offender who set fire to her ex-husband's apartment when he left her—and she considered this to be a completely reasonable response to this injustice. In the movie *Sideways*, one of the characters finds out that her new boyfriend has neglected to tell her that he is about to get married—and she proceeds to bash him in the face with her motorcycle helmet, breaking his nose. Many women feel completely justified threatening to report nonexistent male violence to the police or family or military commanders—as a threat to keep him from reporting hers.

Female offenders will often say things like, *He made me so mad, I had no choice*; or *I was just trying to get his attention, everybody can understand that*; or *Men have all the power, this was just me taking some of it back.* Anything except *I turned to physical violence—I am responsible and it was wrong.*

It is extremely challenging for all of us working with abusive women to respect and validate their legitimate experiences of being victimized (by sexual abuse, physical assault, mistreatment by men)—*and* to make absolutely sure that they do not use these experiences as rationalizations for abuse, violence, retaliation, and payback.

Another pattern of this is evident when women rationalize their abusive behavior of their partners because of a profound sense of entitlement based on their gender expectations. If their expectations about what their partner is supposed to offer them are not met adequately—like providing enough income or giving up his friends or activities to spend his time exclusively with her—entitled women may feel completely justified in payback. And, most disturbingly, they may see nothing wrong with this retaliation and control.

Female entitlement issues also affect our work with these offenders when a woman believes (often quite accurately) that no real consequences will result from her violence toward her partner. She knows that, quite frequently, he won't call the police, because he's too embarrassed or he doesn't really want her to get in trouble. Or she may believe that the police won't really take her assaults seriously because she's "just a woman."

The focus of any treatment program, while including much of the central teachings and skills training of a more typical men's group, must focus more intensely on issues of victimization and trauma in women. This means that we have to be respectful of the power of this previous trauma—but also careful never to collude with women in rationalizing their violence because they have been victimized themselves.

Emotional Self-Regulation

A final note on emotional self-regulation. As discussed in the section What We Now Know About Female Intimate Partner Violence, studies indicate that FIPV offenders have especially high rates of personality disorders, with issues of emotional self-dysregulation (Simmons et al., 2005; Varley Thornton et al., 2010). As a result, these women might be more likely to perpetrate IPV when they are angry or when their needs are not met, which is consistent with theories that individuals might engage in partner violence to regulate negative emotional states (Elmquist et al., 2014). Thus, intervention programs for both men and women should incorporate interventions aimed at increasing emotional self-regulation and effective emotional expression: mindfulness-based interventions, components of acceptance and commitment therapy, dialectical behavioral therapy interventions, and so on. Anything that enhances the appropriate expression and regulation of negative emotions will ultimately reduce the likelihood of IPV.

RULES OF ENGAGEMENT

Assumptions

1. All of us working in the field of domestic violence treatment and prevention recognize that we have one primary mission: to reduce the likelihood—ideally, to eliminate—the risk of future relationship violence.
2. Programs like *The STOP Program for Women Who Abuse* are committed to treating women who have been identified as perpetrators of relationship violence, and doing everything we possibly can to have a positive impact on how they conduct themselves in the future. Our goal is rehabilitation and change.
3. In working with women who have committed these acts of relationship violence, our most effective strategy is to engage the group member to increase the likelihood that she will be receptive to change. If we can't make a connection with her, we can't help her change.

Communicating Respect

It is often difficult for group leaders to listen to the stories of the women in our program dispassionately and compassionately. We all enter this setting with our own values and judgments—let alone personal experiences—and the process of understanding a woman who abuses her partner can provoke difficult emotions.

The women in this program deserve our respect—not, obviously, for the actions they have taken, but rather for the individual stories that have led them to act desperately and destructively. It is very helpful to recognize that many of the women in our groups—like all of us—have become overwhelmed by emotions that they had difficulty handling. And they have lacked the necessary range of skills to handle these emotions in constructive and proactive ways. Although we must always emphasize personal responsibility, it is also essential to recognize our essential similarity and their essential humanity.

It is our belief that when these women become smarter about themselves (more aware of needs, feelings, and motivations) and smarter about options (better skills at self-talk, relaxation, communication, empathy, and problem solving), they will choose otherwise in the future.

PACING AND LEADING

One treatment strategy to help facilitate these goals is called *pacing and leading* (see Pacing and Leading, p. 28). This approach employs the process of carefully mirroring or pacing the experience of the other person—followed by a leading suggestion for a new way to think or act.

This sequence of communicating empathic understanding and respect for the woman's experience, followed by a new perspective or idea, proves very valuable in these groups.

LABELING

It is vital to communicate this message: *We treat the person, not the label.* Stay away from labels that sound like put-downs, such as *offenders, perpetrators, abusers*, and so on. They may be true, and they may be the labels in the legal system, but they do nothing but foster shame—and resistance—in these groups. We want the women to understand that we could put any woman in this group, regardless of what has gone wrong in her relationship patterns, and she would benefit from the approaches used in this treatment model.

INITIAL RESISTANCE

Very frequently group members enter the first session angry and resistant. They complain about being in the group, challenge the group policies, and insist that they will not be talking in these sessions. Unless they are seriously disruptive to the group, it is usually best to respectfully listen to their complaints and then move on. **Power struggles should be avoided whenever possible.** Often women who are the most difficult in the early sessions turn out to be the best group members—as long as they feel respected.

TAKING THINGS SERIOUSLY

Often, the group members will become uncomfortable with the emotionally disturbing discussions that emerge in the group—and they deal with this by laughing or making fun. Sometimes this happens when a group member describes some act of violence toward her partner that she committed because she couldn't get through to him or because he had committed a (perceived) injustice. It can get tiring for the group leaders to lecture the group about how "this is not a funny subject." Often, modeling has the most impact. The group leaders should simply maintain a serious tone themselves. The group members usually get the message quickly.

SYSTEM-BASHING

Just as in male groups, system-bashing also occurs frequently in these groups: bashing the male-dominated court system, Child Protective Services, child custody laws, and so on. These discussions should be short-circuited as quickly as possible. Unlike with men-bashing (see below), however, it is rarely effective to confront these complaints. For one thing, the women may be justified in complaining. For another, it is unproductive to engage in any unnecessary power struggles. The most effective strategy seems to be saying something like this: *You know, you may be right about some of your complaints, but this isn't really the focus of the group sessions. What we need to talk about here is the things you can do differently in your lives.*

MEN-BASHING

Men-bashing often occurs in these group sessions—just as women-bashing shows up in men's groups. In contrast to system-bashing, this should be confronted immediately. Group leaders should point out that generalizations about any social group always turn people into categories rather than individuals. It should be emphasized that it's okay to say that your husband doesn't do enough to help around the house, but not to say that all men are lazy. Furthermore, women who refer to their partner as "that man" or "he" or even "my boyfriend" should be consistently asked to refer to him by name. It can be humanizing to write the name of each of the men who are mentioned in the group on the board as their names come up during each session. Our goal is to make the men in these women's lives as real and human as possible.

User-Friendly Environment

Not only is it important to engage the group members by communicating respect, but this atmosphere of respect is also communicated through the structure of the program and the treatment environment that we design for them. It is also important to recognize the learning styles of the women in our groups and design interventions accordingly.

SHAME-FREE GROUP NAMES

Domestic violence treatment groups should not be called domestic violence treatment groups, at least not as far as the group members are concerned. The names should be neutral, like Group HAWK or Group EAGLE, or positive, like Relationship Skills Training or the STOP Program. These women are very sensitive to being and feeling shamed about their behavior, and the shame experience rarely makes them more amenable to change. Instead, it generates defensiveness and resistance.

SHAME-FRIENDLY GROUP ENVIRONMENT

The discussion in the group should not lead to more shaming than the members are already experiencing. Challenging the group members to recognize the ways in which their behavior has been abusive is one thing; communicating disgust is another. There needs to be room for them to discuss their feelings of shame about their behavior without feeling more of it. The goal is to create a shame-friendly group environment in which shame can be identified and integrated.

INTERACTIVE, ENGAGING TECHNIQUES

Another important design issue for these programs is to make sure that the information which is so vital for their progress is presented in ways that are engaging and user-friendly. Lectures need to be simple and straightforward. The use of video clips, group exercises, demonstrations and role-plays, and humor all enhance the attention span and receptivity of our audience.

OFFERING COUPLES TREATMENT OPTIONS

Many state statutes prohibit any couples treatment options, at least until the offender has fully completed his or her own treatment program. In many cases, this policy makes sense. However, many of the women in our programs know that their partner has also significantly contributed to the violence at home. Even if it is not used in a particular case, the awareness among group members that couples treatment is available communicates the message that the program understands the complexity of many domestic violence situations.

SUBCULTURE-SPECIFIC GROUPS

Again, specific groups may not be possible at all sites, and many programs may object to it on theoretical grounds. However, sometimes women of various subcultures or minority groups (African American, Mexican American, Filipino, lesbian, etc.) feel more comfortable and can be more open in these homogenous groups.

Therapeutic Alliance

Another obvious issue in generating the engagement experience revolves around specific interventions to foster a therapeutic alliance. Years of research about the efficacy of clinical interventions in any setting have taught us that this variable is one of the most essential contributors to any treatment success.

Often this alliance is generated naturally, if the counselor has an intuitive sense of how to foster alliance and if the group member is receptive. Most of you working in this field are already skilled at this. These two brief ideas are intended to remind you of some specific approaches that may enhance this alliance even further.

UNIVERSAL EXPERIENCE

It is very valuable for group members to hear the basic message that "anybody could benefit from this program." In other words, these women are not criminal freaks. They are people who—like all of us—have failed sometimes in handling the complexities of love relationships. Without in any way minimizing the seriousness and tragedy of their offenses, it is still very treatment-friendly to make it clear that the group leaders, too, could benefit from going through a program like this which examines relationship assumptions and relationship behavior.

PREGROUP PREPARATION

As Yalom (1995) has indicated, one of the most valuable contributors to the success of brief group therapies is the use of appropriate pregroup preparation. This helps foster the alliance, right off the bat, necessary for successful group performance. The orientation session of *The STOP Program for Women Who Abuse*, Second Edition, is designed with exactly these principles in mind. We want to have the new, unsure, and defensive group member form an alliance with the group leader(s) without competition from the rest of the group.

STAGES OF CHANGE AND MOTIVATIONAL INTERVIEWING

The following article is adapted with permission from the work of Susan Storm, MS, MFT, who has been working in the field of criminal justice for over 25 years. She has worked in both juvenile and adult probation as an officer, a supervisor, and a director, and was instrumental in bringing evidence-based practices to her department in the 1990s.

The Stages of Change model—and the techniques of Motivational Interviewing that have emerged from this model—are very valuable in working with domestic violence offenders, both male and female. This paradigm, originally developed by developed by Prochaska and DiClemente (1984) for treating addictions, is based on the observation that we all go through stages whenever we try to make changes in our lives. This is true for criminal populations as well as the rest of us making any change in our established routine.

Stages Of Change

STAGE 1: PRECONTEMPLATION

The first stage is called Precontemplation. As the word implies, it's a state of consciousness in which a person has no awareness that they want to, need to, or should change some behavior in their lives. We used to use the word *denial* to describe someone who didn't clearly see the uselessness of their behavior, but that term is not really adequate to describe the thought process involved, and its connotation is negative, rather than observational:

- when an overweight person is eating a hot fudge sundae without any concern about fat and calorie content;
- when a smoker is lighting a cigarette without any thought of health issues like cancer, heart attacks, or strokes;
- when an FIPV offender abuses her partner without thinking about her partner's welfare or the consequences this will have for her life and her family.

FEMALE IPV OFFENDER: *I don't have a problem with violence—so I have no interest in changing my behavior.*

STAGE 2: CONTEMPLATION

The second stage of the thought process leading to change is Contemplation. During this stage we're generally giving some thought to change, but dismiss our concerns and continue with our routine behavior. It's a pivotal point that primes the person for action, since the person is beginning to weigh both sides of their behavior and decide what to do next.

This is a time when ambivalence is apparent, as a woman thinks, "I want to and at the same time I don't want to":

- when the overweight person who orders the sundae says, "I should probably eat fruit instead of this, but I really want the ice cream, so this time I'm having it";
- when the smoker thinks, "I know this is really bad for my health" but lights up anyway;
- when the woman assaulting her husband thinks, "I hope I don't get caught" but continues to scratch his face when she feels jealous.

FEMALE IPV OFFENDER: *I realize I might have a problem with violence—but I'm not sure I want to do anything about it yet—maybe later.*

STAGE 3: PREPARATION (OR DETERMINATION)

The third stage of change is called Preparation (or Determination). During this stage, a person gets past their unconsciousness and past some of their ambivalence—and begins to actually consider the possibility of a behavioral change. They may be learning about the consequences of their behaviors, reading, talking to people, and doing their own sort of research on the subject. Note that in each example given, the person is not yet changing behavior, but moving in that direction:

- the overweight person saying, "Tomorrow I'm going to begin a diet, so this is the last hot fudge sundae I'll have for a long time";
- the smoker who says, "I've had enough of this. Cigarettes are harmful and I'm going to stop smoking";
- the abuser who says, "I can't keep doing this—I'm going to lose my marriage and I may end up in jail."

FEMALE IPV OFFENDER: *I know now that I have a problem with violence—and I have to do something about this so I can have a better life and better relationships.*

STAGE 4: ACTION

The next stage is Action. This is when a person takes some real action toward behavior change. They're not just thinking about it or deciding if they should change—they're actually committed to changing behavior:

- the overweight person who orders the salad for lunch and then goes to the gym;
- the smoker who throws his last pack of cigarettes in the trash;
- the abuser who takes a time-out instead of physically assaulting his or her partner.

FEMALE IPV OFFENDER: *I realize now that my abusive behavior is unacceptable, and I will not allow myself to return to it. I will commit myself to groups, therapy, spiritual guidance, books, and good people—anything to help me make these changes.*

STAGE 5: MAINTENANCE

Unfortunately, the researchers found that Action is not always the end of the process. The next stage is Maintenance. At this stage the person maintains their new behavior for at least six months and is in the process of working on long-term change.

For some people, that's the end of the process. They change behaviors and never look back. For most of us, however, it's hard. Most people relapse at least once when making a difficult behavioral change:

- a successful dieter who feels depressed and eats "everything in the refrigerator" one night;
- a former smoker who goes to a party, has a drink, and decides to have a cigarette too;
- a former batterer who gets angry at her girlfriend and threatens her.

FEMALE IPV OFFENDER: *I realize that it's going to take a lot of work, over a long period of time, to maintain these changes and keep growing. I have to surround myself with the right people, and I have to watch very carefully for warning signs that I might be slipping.*

Motivational Interviewing

Before we look at the principles and skills used in Motivational Interviewing, think about your own experience with offenders. What works, at least sometimes, in motivating an offender to understand the need for change, desire change, and initiate the process of change?

Miller and Rollnick (1991) began their research in order to determine the best methods to move people through the Stages of Change. By looking at techniques used by those counseling drug addicts, they noticed that certain behaviors on the part of the counselor caused people to become resistant to change. What they saw was that ordering, demanding, moralizing, threatening, shaming, and other confrontational techniques failed, and that replacing these with successful techniques made a difference in success rates.

They defined their approaches as a directive, client-centered counseling style for helping clients explore and resolve ambivalence about behavior change.

The first principle is to *develop discrepancies* when you see or hear them. This is particularly useful when helping the offender see that a particular behavior is actually preventing her from achieving something she desires. For example, a person who wants to join the military isn't doing themselves any favors by continually getting arrested and convicted of crimes. And a juvenile who wants to be a teacher someday is not considering how a juvenile record could affect his ability to pursue that goal.

The purpose of developing discrepancies is to point out how certain behaviors prevent the offender from achieving her goals so she can make better choices.

The second principle is to *express empathy*. This establishes a rapport that lets the offender know we're working together, we hear what she's saying, and we're supportive of her journey through change. Empathic responses, such as, "I bet that was disruptive to your life," after she says, "I went to jail again last week," let her know you can appreciate her situation, and you understand the implications.

The purpose of expressing empathy is to let the offender know you hear and you understand.

The third principle in Motivational Interviewing is to *avoid argumentation*. It's sometimes easy to get into an argument with an offender who doesn't seem to be thinking or behaving in a prosocial way. But this principle states that power struggles aren't conducive to changing behaviors; instead, they simply add to a person's resistance to change. Learning how to avoid arguments and motivate an offender to voice and act on prosocial values is the goal here.

The rationale for avoiding argumentation is that arguments increase resistance, and an offender is less likely to make behavioral changes.

Rolling with resistance is the fourth principle of Motivational Interviewing. This concept is similar to avoiding argumentation. It teaches us to listen more carefully to her reasoning in order to gain insight into her thinking process if she is resistant. It may also be a time to change subjects to one that is less threatening to defuse the resistance (of course you need to come back to the relevant topic a bit later). Often, just using a reflective response, such as, "This must be hard for you," is enough to let her know you're listening and not judging.

The purpose of rolling with resistance is to help the offender remove herself from a position in which she feels it's necessary to defend herself and continue to resist change.

The last principle is *support self-efficacy*. This means letting the offender know that you believe she has the ability to make better choices in life if additional information and resources are provided. Sometimes the offender needs time, explanations, counseling, small-step processes, and information that she somehow missed along the way. Your assistance in obtaining these important pieces, along with your belief that they will make a difference, is crucial in the motivational process.

The purpose of supporting self-efficacy is to let the offender know that with more information, you believe she has the ability to make better choices in her life.

Motivational Interviewing Skills

Here are the relatively simple techniques used in Motivational Interviewing.

The first technique is to ask *open-ended questions* rather than closed questions. Open-ended questions cannot be answered with a *yes* or *no* and cannot be answered with one word. They are intended to make the offender open up a bit and begin to explore her thought process with you. They will also allow you to gather more information (particularly about how she thinks) than you would normally get with closed questions.

Open-ended questions begin with words like:

- *Tell me about . . .*
- *What happened when . . .*
- *What do you think about . . .*

- *Explain to me about . . .*
- *Why did you . . .*
- *How did you . . .*

As you can see, these questions require some thinking and cognitive exploration on the offender's part. They will start to reveal not only content, but where her thinking puts her in the Stages of Change.

Open-ended questions sound like this:

- *Tell me what you think will happen if you go to prison again.*
- *Explain what you'd like to do about that.*
- *What do you think it would be like if you never drank alcohol again?*

The second technique used in Motivational Interviewing is *affirmations*. People are motivated by praise or recognition, and these statements are metaphorically giving offenders a pat on the back for thinking, expressing, or doing something prosocial. They are also used to amplify strengths and show respect. In addition, these affirmations can help deflect resistance.

Affirmations sound like this:

- *That's great* (said after a client tells you she got a job).
- *Good for you* (said after a client tells you she took a time-out instead of acting on her anger).
- *You look nice today* (said when a client comes into your office neat and clean).

The third strategic skill in Motivational Interviewing is the use of *reflections*. This is simply listening to what your client is saying and then repeating back what you heard—either verbatim or in different words. It shows her that you're listening, gives her the opportunity to correct you if you didn't understand her intent, and gives her a chance to hear something about herself that perhaps she's never actually realized before.

Reflective statements sound like these:

- *You really moved around a lot after your divorce* (said after someone tells you that she lived in five different apartments during the year following her divorce).
- *It sounds like you're depressed* (said after someone tells you she's been crying all day, can't eat, and feels like life isn't turning out like she thought it would).
- *You're really angry and don't think you were treated fairly* (said after someone tells you how much she hates the way the court treated her).

And the last skill used in Motivational Interview is *summarization*. This is very similar to reflections, except that it's used after someone gives you a string of information that you want to summarize. Usually we use this after at least three pieces of information have been shared, and it's a good skill to have when you want to change the focus of your conversation and sum up what you've talked about so far.

Summarization statements sound like this:

- *Let's see if I have this right: You drank alcohol when you were young, started using hard drugs when you were in your late 20s, and now you say you've been clean and sober over 10 years* (said after someone spends 10 minutes giving a rundown of her drug and alcohol use).
- *You want to control your temper, but you're afraid your friends will get you all stirred up, and you don't know who to hang out with if you stop associating with those friends* (said after an offender expresses ambivalence about her ability to remain nonabusive in the future).

THE CONTEXT OF COMPETENCE

Generating the context of competence is an approach based on principles for solution-focused therapies (O'Hanlon & Weiner-Davis, 1989). Based on the original work of Milton Erickson, these solution-focused approaches insist on emphasizing the inherent strengths in the individual or in the family system, rather than focusing exclusively on the deficits, problems, or failures. The philosophy of the context of competence is to "catch yourself doing something right." Even when people have made mistakes or behaved destructively in their relationships, it is very valuable to still identify the parts that went right—and build on these strengths.

This is a problem-solving approach to difficulties that concentrates more on finding effective ways to meet challenges rather than analyzing all the reasons why someone finds herself in these difficulties (which can be very interesting, but generally does not bring about change). It can be applied to a wide range of problems and challenges, and it is not limited to any one theoretical approach.

Even if you never use any of the specific techniques or strategies of solution-focused therapies in your group programs, it is extremely valuable to help create the context of competence atmosphere. Many of the women in our domestic violence programs experience intense levels of shame and failure. This not an excuse for abuse—it is just a psychological reality. If our dominant goal is to prevent future relationship violence, then one of our most valuable strategies is to help bring out their best qualities—using whatever it takes to help them get there.

Essentially, we are sending women the message that we believe they are fully capable of handling their relationships more successfully. We want to identify those successes very clearly and reward them for doing things right—while never, of course, minimizing or ignoring doing things wrong.

Even the very first question on the Weekly Check-In (see p. 41) about reporting weekly successes is a direct reflection of the context of competence orientation.

In analyzing a relationship problem, it is also very helpful to identify the strengths that already exist.

PAST SUCCESS: *What have you done in the past that was successful?*

POSITIVE EXCEPTIONS: *Even though you argue a lot about money, when are you able to talk about money without arguing?*

COPING STATEMENTS: *What do you already know about how to handle these issues successfully?*

SCALING QUESTIONS: *I know you still bicker and criticize each other. But pay attention to times when it's happening less frequently (or doesn't last as long, or never gets as bad as it used to).*

Typical questions that help generate the context of competence are the following:

- *How will we know when you've really been successful with the STOP Program?*
- *After you finish coming here, what kind of changes do you think you'll continue to make in your life?*
- *What's the first sign you'll be able to notice that the STOP Program has been helpful to you?*
- *What's the first sign others will be able to see that the STOP Program has been helpful to you?*
- *If you've experienced similar problems before, how did you deal with them?*
- *Tell us about one of the times when you started to lose it—but you stopped it before it went too far.*
- *Can you remember a time recently when you pleasantly surprised yourself or did something out of character that pleased you?*
- *Even though you yelled at your boyfriend, it sounds like you were able to stop yourself from threatening him or becoming physical. How were you successful at stopping yourself here?*
- *Even though you had a big blowout, it sounds like the two of you were able to end it pretty quickly—and after about an hour it was pretty much over. How were the two of you successful at recovering so quickly?*

PACING AND LEADING

One strategy to bypass the inherent defensiveness of the domestic violence offenders in our programs is called *pacing and leading*. This approach, originating from the work of Milton Erickson and further developed by neo-Ericksonian practitioners (Erickson & Rossi, 1979; Gilligan, 1987), carefully mirrors the experience of the other person—followed by a leading suggestion for a new way to think or act. Based on Erickson's original work with indirect, naturalistic hypnotherapy, pacing means first developing empathy and rapport for the other person's experience by careful delineation—prior to making any correction or suggestion, prior to fostering a new perspective, prior to guiding a new behavior.

> STEP ONE: *Offer mirroring responses that confirm the person's experience.*
>
> STEP TWO: *Then—and only then—lead him or her into some new ways of thinking, feeling, or behaving.*

In domestic violence groups, *pacing* means carefully reflecting back an understanding of a woman's experience:

- *When Michael was talking to this other girl at the party, you must have felt really threatened, like something very important was being taken away from you.*
- *And you must have felt betrayed, like, "How can he do this to me?"*
- *Plus it was in front of other people, and your pride was at stake.*
- *And you felt powerless, probably thinking, "I have to* do *something about this right now."*
- *You probably felt it all through your body.*
- *And it felt awful.*
- *And you didn't know what to do.*
- *It makes sense that you would feel this way, and that you would feel this urge to try to do* something *to feel powerful again.*

Then, and only then, comes the *lead*:

- *And at that point, probably the most* powerful *thing to do would be to remember that you get insecure in these situations, and that it doesn't always mean that Michael is* doing *something to you. And to remember that you have ways to talk to him about it afterward. You can let him know what you need from him.*

There are three kinds of mistakes you can make in pacing and leading:

> IMPROPER PACING: *If you tell someone that they must be very anxious right now, and they are not, then the pacing is off-base.*

INSUFFICIENT PACING: *If you make a few pacing statements and the person is still very guarded and mistrusting, it may mean that you need to spend more time with the pacing process.*

IMPROPER LEAD: *Even though you may have paced very accurately and successfully, your lead suggestion may be something that doesn't make sense or feels offensive in some way to the person.*

When in doubt, return to pacing. It is hard to go wrong by doing this.

In the situation above, the group leader could have simply stepped in with the obvious lead—but without proper pacing, the likely response for the group member would have been something like: *You don't know what it's like to have him treat me like this!* Without pacing, you lack emotional credibility. With pacing, the person is more likely to feel understood and then more receptive to the value of the advice, guidance, or correction.

PART II

PROGRAM INFORMATION

PROGRAM NOTES

The STOP Program for Women Who Abuse utilizes the core elements of the original *STOP Program* (for men), which apply universally to all relationships—along with many special features that are specifically designed for women.

1. PROGRAM DESIGN: This manual is designed for use in a civilian or military setting as part of an open-ended 26-week group treatment program for female domestic violence offenders, but the 26-session format also makes it suitable for programs with 52 weekly sessions by simply repeating the 26-session cycle. In order to maintain fidelity to the program model, all group members must attend 26 sessions. If the program is condensed into fewer sessions, group members cannot claim to have successfully completed the STOP Program.

2. SESSION STRUCTURE: Each session is designed for a two-hour period, with a 10-minute break in the middle. All group sessions begin with review of homework from the previous session, plus a brief mindfulness and gratitude ritual, followed by a review of the Weekly Check-In (see p. 41) which the group members must fill out prior to the beginning of group. The group leaders should briefly review these check-ins to alert them to any specific issues which should be covered in that session.

Special Guideline: In the typical STOP Program men's domestic violence group, the open-ended group therapy session typically takes place in the first hour, with the more didactic psychoeducational program in the second hour after the break. However, we have discovered that it is usually much more effective to reverse the order in the female offender groups—because, typically, once these women get going with the more open-ended discussion, they do not want to stop. They often offer strong resistance to the group leaders when it is time to switch over to more didactic material.

So a more effective strategy based on the Premack principle ("You've got to eat your vegetables first, and then you can have dessert") is to switch the order for the female offender groups: psychoeducational lesson in the first half, then the open-ended group discussion in the second half.

3. HANDOUTS: The group members in this program use *The STOP Program for Women: Homework and Handouts*, which includes all of the forms, exercises, and homework assignments for the sessions and the additional material.

PLEASE NOTE: ALL GROUP MEMBERS MUST HAVE THEIR OWN PERSONAL ORIGINAL COPY OF *Homework and Handouts*— COPYING THESE FORMS IS A VIOLATION OF COPYRIGHT LAWS.

4. TEACHING METHODS: These sessions are designed to be psychoeducational, with lecture, demonstration, and role-playing, as well as personal group discussion. Both the educational and the psychological are essential for the program's success. In order for group members to properly learn the skills and techniques, group discussion of personal experiences and specific applications is encouraged.

5. EVALUATION FORM: The evaluation form that you will be using to evaluate group members' performance should be previewed at intake with the group member. Explain each of the criteria. It is also helpful to review these items in the group format. As you review each item, ask at least one group member to assess her own performance in this area. This is an excellent opportunity to offer genuine feedback, bolster self-esteem, and stimulate increased mutual support from group members.

NOTE: Your agency might use a different evaluation form than the sample included in *The STOP Program for Women Who Abuse,* Second Edition, Group Leader's Manual.

6. HOMEWORK: Homework is regularly assigned throughout these sessions. All homework should be reviewed early in each session. It is usually not necessary (and too time consuming) to carefully review each group member's homework in each session. However, it is essential to at least review one or two examples of the homework and to conduct a quick visual check to make sure all group members have completed the work. Group members will quickly recognize if homework is not taken seriously—they will not take it seriously either.

NOTE: We recommend that any failure to complete homework be noted in the group member's chart, and three homework failures should trigger a letter back to the referring agency about noncompliance.

7. ORIENTATION SESSIONS: Several forms are included for meeting with new group members prior to their first group session. Research has indicated that this pre-group preparation is extremely valuable in setting the stage for successful treatment.

8. NEW MEMBER SESSIONS: If possible, new group members should only be admitted during one session each month. In other words, there will be one session per month in each group during which new members will be integrated; the remaining sessions each month will not be disrupted by new admissions.

When new members are entering the group, the STOP Program model is to engage in a brief "getting to know you" exercise (described in the New Member Session information) and to review one of two exercises with the group: House of Abuse or Time-Out. In other words, if you review House of Abuse in the January New Member Session, you will review Time-Out in February—then House of Abuse again in March, and so on. This information is so central to our work that it bears repeating for the veteran group members, who actually get it better and better with every repetition.

The material of the New Member Session is not a replacement for the scheduled material in the sessions. It should be integrated into the overall format of that session as much as possible.

9. EXIT SESSION: When an individual group member is within three or four sessions of completing her program, she should go through the Exit exercises (Most Violent/Most Disturbing Incident). All group members will thus have witnessed a number of these successful "graduations" by the time it's their turn.

The material of the Exit Session is not a replacement for the scheduled material in the sessions. It should be integrated into the overall format of that session as much as possible.

10. STANDARD FORMS: Several standard forms are included for use in the programs. Each form may be used as is, adapted for the needs of the particular program, or abandoned completely. The key forms are:

- *Weekly Check-In*
- *Evaluation Form*

YOU HAVE FULL PERMISSION TO COPY THESE STANDARD FORMS FOR GROUP USE.

11. THE FIFTEEN COMMANDMENTS OF STOP: The Fifteen Commandments of STOP (see The Fifteen Commandments of STOP handout) are central themes that run through all the treatment sessions, even if there are no specific lectures devoted to them. A poster-size version of these commandments should be posted on the group room walls. Whenever a subject related to any of the commandments emerges in the group discussion, it is helpful to interrupt, point to the poster, and ask someone to read aloud the relevant commandment. The Fifteen Commandments of STOP should be reviewed in the initial orientation session.

12. WOMEN IN SAME-SEX RELATIONSHIPS: Historically, straight and gay offenders have been treated separately in both men's and women's groups. However, in recent years many programs have experimented with integrating heterosexual and same-sex or bisexual offenders (and even transgender offenders who identify as female) in the same group—with very promising results. Some of the focus on male-female gender roles may not apply, but the central themes of the STOP Program (and the experience of being female) definitely do.

Please note that many of the examples and vignettes in The STOP Program for Women Who Abuse, Second Edition, now use the term partner and alternately refer to one's partner as him or her, to make this more user-friendly to both straight and gay group members.

13. MALE AND FEMALE COFACILITATORS: The optimal format for leading a group involves a male and female cofacilitator team. The group members benefit from a counseling relationship with therapists of both genders. We have generally found it valuable for the female coleader to take the lead when confronting any group members regarding male-bashing or negative generalizations about men. This models a female consciousness about male-female politics—which sounds different when a male appears to be merely defending himself or his gender. The cofacilitator team can also effectively model respectful disagreement and conflict resolution.

Please do not take this as a criticism of programs that run groups with single group leaders or with two women or even two men. These can all work just fine. However, if funding, resources, and personnel allow, then this male-female team design is optimal.

14. TREATMENT FAILURE (see Provisional Status Policy): If any group member is showing clear signs that treatment is not progressing successfully, she should be confronted about her behavior and informed that there is a problem as early as possible in the treatment program. We usually expect to be able to flag these problems by Week 4 or 5. It is unfair to inform a group member after 13 sessions that we have decided she is not benefiting from the program (unless some unexpected event, like a reabuse, has suddenly taken place). Indications of treatment failure include belligerent attitudes, refusal to do any homework, refusal to participate, consistent verbal aggression when discussing males, and so on.

15. PROGRAM LIMITATIONS: When introducing new skills (such as Asking for Change or Time-Out) to the group members, it is very important to emphasize that there is no guarantee that these skills will always bring about a positive outcome. In fact, there are times when being assertive or using active listening or I-messages is not the best course. The message we should send is that usually these are the most respectful forms of communication, and respectful communication is generally the most effective in the long run.

16. *THE STOP PROGRAM FOR WOMEN WHO ABUSE* LIMITATIONS: Many aspects of conducting a comprehensive domestic violence treatment program are not included in this manual: supporting victims, intake and assessment procedures, coordinating efforts with civilian court systems and other agencies, selecting and supervising staff members, and so on. We strongly recommend that agencies develop thorough systems and policies for the wider range of services in treating domestic violence. This manual is designed only to treat women who have committed some form of substantiated psychological and/or physical act or acts of abuse against their partners.

VIDEO INFORMATION

URLs retrieved July 2023

1. Many of these scenes are available on YouTube, and the URL is noted alongside each scene below.
2. Other scenes are available by purchasing the DVD from Amazon or any other seller, and are also available via streaming. These are marked below with the word "PURCHASE." The specific timing of the scene is noted below. The exact timing of the specific video clips may vary on different DVD players.
3. Program facilitators are strongly encouraged to use their own video clips to specifically illustrate key points in this program if they find them useful. However, only brief video clips should be used—group members should never be stuck in a room to watch a 1-hour or 2-hour video. This is not the best use of group time.

THE STOP PROGRAM—For Women Who Abuse Videos

DVDs AVAILABLE FROM AMAZON AND OTHER OUTLETS/ALSO AVAILABLE VIA STREAMING

Session #5

- *Sideways* (The female assault scene begins at 1:35:04 and ends at 1:36:18 when man says "Keep it elevated")

Session #4

- *When A Man Loves A Woman* (begins at 30:54 when woman gets out of the cab, ends at 35:40 after father tells daughter that he is sending someone over to help)

Session #6

- *I, Tonya (*Abuse by mother begins at 23:43 and ends at 25:21 and begins again at 55:05 and ends at 57:17, then couple assault scene begins at 44:45 and ends at 45:45)

Session #16

- *In Treatment, Season 1* (HBO series), Jake and Amy—Week One (begins just before wife walks up to the door at 6:20 and ends after husband makes comment about her hemorrhoids at 16:23)

Session #26

- *The Great Santini (*Kids witnessing spouse abuse begins at 1:28:29 and ends at 1:29:57)

DVD AVAILABLE FROM SPECIFIC OUTLETS

https://studio.youtube.com/video/F5d_6QCRX8c/editMen
Full *Men Don't Tell* DVD available from https://www.raredvds.biz/Men_Don_t_Tell_DVD_1993_Peter_Strauss_p/men_dont_tell.htm
(also available on YouTube at https://www.youtube.com/watch?v=U_gLDF2dGLY)

- ***Session #3*** Female projecting blame (begins at 28:12 and ends at 30:20 on DVD or 25:20-28:14 on YouTube)
- ***Session #15*** Male keeping secrets *(*begins at 13:44 and ends at 16:11 on DVD or 14:18-16:47 on YouTube + 42:50-46:54 on DVD or 40:00-44:04 on YouTube)
- ***Session #23*** Female taking responsibility (begins at 1:41:53 and ends at 1:45:31 on DVD or 1:27:50-1:31:53 on YouTube)

AVAILABLE FROM YOUTUBE

Session #1 When Women Abuse Men

- https://www.youtube.com/watch?v=gZVJoSP4UEU&feature=youtu.be)

Session #5 Blame & Accountability

- https://www.youtube.com/watch?v=RZWf2_2L2v8

Session #10 The Power of Empathy

- https://www.youtube.com/watch?v=1Evwgu369Jw

Session #22 When Your Partner Doesn't Trust You

- https://www.youtube.com/watch?v=K9hznPEcRSg

Session #26 First Impressions: Exposure to Violence and a Child's Developing Brain

- https://www.youtube.com/watch?v=eEEVKDW5NDc

PROVISIONAL STATUS POLICY
(Group Leader's Version)

The following are grounds for group members to be placed on Provisional Status in the STOP Program (leading to possible termination). These behaviors are in addition to activity that takes place outside of the group sessions, such as acts of violence, repeated drug or alcohol problems, or failure to attend group:

1. **Consistently** putting down men or minimizing violence
2. **Persistent** disruptive or oppositional behavior in group
3. **Consistent** projection of blame for relationship problems without self-examination
4. **Consistent** lack of participation in group, including failure to complete homework assignments
5. **Consistent** pattern of "telling stories" (bragging or showing off) about controlling, abusive, or violent behavior with little or no signs of remorse

If the group member is deemed to be appropriate for Provisional Status based on the criteria above or other behaviors deemed possible grounds for failure, the following steps should be taken:

1. Discuss these concerns directly with her. Indicate exactly what you need to see in the future for her to continue in the program. Indicate when her behavior will be reviewed again (usually 1 to 3 weeks). Depending on clinical judgment, this discussion can take place privately or in the group itself.
2. Follow up with group member and give feedback indicating either her success in meeting program standards or informing her that you are recommending termination from the program.

It is our policy to attempt to engage group members in the treatment process and to help them correct unacceptable behaviors if possible. Strategies for intervening when group members are engaging in these behaviors include the following:

1. At first, give the benefit of the doubt and assume ignorance: *You may not be aware of this, but . . .* or *I don't think you realize how this comes across, but . . .*

2. Try to keep the interventions as benign and respectful as possible. Remember that these women are feeling defensive, and they are often testing us to see what they can get away with.
3. As much as possible, state the rules as clearly and simply as possible.
4. Employ pacing and leading whenever possible. Make sure that the group member feels that her point is recognized and respected even if you are correcting her behavior. Continue to remind the group members that, although their complaints about their partners, job, or the legal system may be valid, the purpose of this group is to examine ourselves.
5. If a problem behavior is developing, catch it as early as possible in the group member's treatment. Patterns of problem behavior should be noted and confronted no later than sessions 4 or 5 for an individual group member. For example, make a comment the first time someone talks about the way "all men" are.
6. However, be careful about confronting problem behavior too early. Many of these women need to have room to be defensive and oppositional early on and often come around on their own.
7. If you are feeling intimidated by a nucleus of group members who are being disruptive, discuss this with colleagues. In these situations, it is often wise to meet privately with problem group members to enlist their alliance with the group goals. It also helps to issue a general (not aimed at a single person) statement to the group about what you expect from the group.
8. If one member is being difficult, you may choose to discuss this in the group, so that other group members can see that someone is taking charge of the direction of the group. Other members also may have valuable feedback for this group member. However, the strategies for handling these situations are clinical, case-by-case decisions.
9. Remember that you are fully empowered to recommend that a group member be terminated from group. This does not represent a failure of the program or the group leaders.

THE STOP PROGRAM FOR WOMEN: WEEKLY CHECK-IN

Handout (page 9 in *Handouts & Homework*)

Name ______________________ Date ______________________

1. **SUCCESS.** Describe one way in the past week in which you successfully kept yourself from being aggressive or successfully used something you learned in group. The success can be large or small. This is a chance to pat yourself on the back.

   What was the situation?

   What might you have done in the past?

   What did you do right?

Calmly stood up for my rights		Told myself to relax		Took a Time-Out	
Expressed my feelings responsibly		Changed my self-talk		Other	

2. **SUBSTANCE USE.** Please remember that the first question the court, probation officer, or other referring agency will ask, when they receive knowledge that you have used, is: "Was the treatment provider aware of this?" If we were aware of it, we can tell them, "Yes, and here is what we're doing to help him or her." Over the course of the last week did you use any of the following?

Alcohol (only report if you are prohibited from drinking as part of your probation mandate)		Methamphetamine		Cocaine	

If you answered *yes* to any of the above, please describe the circumstances, and the thought you used that gave you permission. ______________________________

____

____

____

3. **PROBLEM SITUATION.** Describe one way in the past week in which you did not handle an interpersonal situation well.

   What was the situation?

   How upset did you feel?

0	10	20	30	40	50	60	70	80	90	100
Not at All Upset					Upset					Extremely Upset

   How did you respond?

4. **AGGRESSION.** Did you become verbally or physically aggressive toward anyone in the past week (including threats and damage to property)?

Slapping		Kicking		Grabbing/Restraining	
Punching/Hitting		Property Destruction		Throwing Things	
Verbal/Emotional Abuse		Sexual Abuse		Other	

   What would you do in a similar situation in the future to avoid becoming aggressive?

5. **HOMEWORK.** Did you complete homework for the week?

   Yes _____ No _____ None Assigned _____

PLEASE NOTE:
YOU HAVE FULL PERMISSION TO COPY THIS FORM FOR GROUP USE.

GUT CHECK QUESTIONNAIRE

Handout (page 11 in *Handouts & Homework*)

Adapted with permission from Dutton, D. G. (1998). The abusive personality: Violence and control in intimate relationships. New York: Guilford Press.

Name ______________________ Date ______________________

Answer each of these questions as honestly as you can. None of these answers will be shared with the group without your consent. Use a number from 1 to 10, with 1 being lowest and 10 being highest. When answering questions 4, 5, and 6, remember that the purpose of this is simply to offer some valuable feedback to one of your peers. Most of us have trouble seeing ourselves clearly without honest feedback from others who care about us.

1. How honest am I being in the group? *(Not at all/Completely)* _____ (1–10)
2. How much effort am I putting into the group? *(Not at all/Completely)* _____ (1–10)
3. How much feedback am I giving to others in the group? *(Not at all/Completely)* _____ (1–10)
4. Who do I know the most/least in the group?

   Most ______________________

   Least ______________________
5. Who is acknowledging responsibility for her relationship problems most in the group?

   Most ______________________
6. Who is being the most emotionally honest in the group?

   Most ______________________
7. How much am I getting out of the group?

1	2	3	4	5	6	7	8	9	10
Nothing		A little		Some value			A lot		Very much

STOP PROGRAM: EVALUATION FORM

Handout (page 12 in *Handouts & Homework*)

This sample form is to be completed at the end of sessions 13, 26, 39, and 52 (for a 52-week program), as well as any other time when there are special recommendations or concerns.

Group member's name: ______________________________

Group leaders' names: ______________________________

____

Group attended: ____________________ Dates: __________ to __________

Total # sessions attended: ______ Date of report: ____________

Please evaluate the group member on all the scales listed below. The norm group should be the overall population of group members at this stage of treatment. Give a 1 for the lowest score on each item and a 9 for the highest score, with any number in between that best describes your assessment.

PARTICIPATION

No personal self-disclosure	1 2 3 4 5 6 7 8 9	Appropriate self-disclosure
Defensive	1 2 3 4 5 6 7 8 9	Very open to feedback
Feedback aggressive/destructive	1 2 3 4 5 6 7 8 9	Feedback constructive
Does not complete homework	1 2 3 4 5 6 7 8 9	Completes homework

BEHAVIOR

Poor ability expressing feelings	1 2 3 4 5 6 7 8 9	Excellent ability
Does not recognize responsibility for family violence	1 2 3 4 5 6 7 8 9	Recognizes responsibility
Poor control over impulses and behavior	1 2 3 4 5 6 7 8 9	Good control
Minimal empathy/concern for victim or other family members	1 2 3 4 5 6 7 8 9	Excellent empathy/concern
Little self-awareness of buildup of tension or emotional needs	1 2 3 4 5 6 7 8 9	Excellent self-awareness
Poor assertive expression of needs and feelings	1 2 3 4 5 6 7 8 9	Excellent assertiveness

EVALUATION FORM - PAGE 2

Handout (page 13 in *Handouts & Homework*)

Please rate the group member's overall progress, **as compared to the overall population of group members at this stage of treatment.** Rate on a scale of 1–9, with 1 as no improvement and 9 as outstanding improvement.

1 2 3 4 5 6 7 8 9 N/A

At this time, check the box if you recommend either of the following:

Probation: ______________

Termination from program: ______________

COMMENTS

____

____

____

____

____

____

____

Group leader signature ____

Group leader signature ____

TREATMENT EXPECTATIONS

Here are some basic guidelines about what treatment programs typically expect from group members at various stages of their treatment. These expectations are based on a 52-week program and may be adapted depending on length of treatment.

Treatment Expectations, Weeks 1–12

1. PARTICIPATION: Arrives on time, attentive, asks questions, constructive contribution to group discussions, is able to describe incident that brought him/her to program.
2. ATTITUDE: Uses respectful language, demonstrates gender respect, respect for group process and other members, accountability for actions.
3. HOMEWORK: Completed as assigned, shows thought and effort.
4. BASIC SKILLS: Uses I statements, reports appropriate use of time-outs, identifies red flags, uses listening skills.

Treatment Expectations, Weeks 13–25

1. PARTICIPATION: Arrives on time, attentive, asks questions, constructive contribution to group discussions, willingness to voluntarily participate.
2. ATTITUDE: Uses respectful language, demonstrates gender respect, respect for group process and other members, accountability for actions.
3. HOMEWORK: Completed as assigned, shows thought and effort.
4. BASIC SKILLS: Uses I statements, reports appropriate use of time-outs, identifies red flags, uses listening skills.
5. ADVANCED SKILLS: Reflective listening, utilizes compromise and negotiation tools, identifies personal strengths and weaknesses (positive change and areas of concern), uses noncontrolling communication.

Treatment Expectations, Weeks 26–39

1. PARTICIPATION: Arrives on time, attentive, asks questions, constructive contribution to group discussions, willingness to voluntarily participate, initiates constructive dialogue, appropriately challenges others.

2. ATTITUDE: Uses respectful language, demonstrates gender respect, respect for group process and other members, accountability for actions, consistent modeling of positive changes in behavior and attitude.
3. HOMEWORK: Completed as assigned, shows better-developed thought and effort.
4. BASIC SKILLS: Consistent use of I statements, reports appropriate use of time-outs, identifies red flags, uses listening skills.
5. ADVANCED SKILLS: Consistent use and modeling of skills: reflective listening, utilizing compromise and negotiation tools, identifying personal strengths and weaknesses (positive change and areas of concern), uses noncontrolling communication. Reports use of new skills in current relationships.

Treatment Expectations, Weeks 40–52

1. PARTICIPATION: Arrives on time, consistently attentive, asks questions, constructive contribution to group discussions, willingness to voluntarily participate, initiates constructive dialogue, appropriately challenges others.
2. ATTITUDE: Uses respectful language, demonstrates gender respect, respect for group process and other members, accountability for actions, consistent modeling of positive changes in behavior and attitude, maintains self-confidence and commitment to nonviolence.
3. HOMEWORK: Completed as assigned, shows better-developed thought and effort, approved relapse prevention plan accomplished.
4. BASIC SKILLS: Maintains consistent use of I statements, reports appropriate use of time-outs, identifies red flags, uses listening skills.
5. ADVANCED SKILLS: Consistent use and modeling of skills: reflective listening, utilizing compromise and negotiation tools, identifying personal strengths and weaknesses (positive change and areas of concern), uses noncontrolling communication. Positive modeling for other group members; demonstrates empathy for victim, children, and others.

PART III

ORIENTATION MATERIALS

WELCOME!

Welcome to the STOP Program for Women. You are here because of a report indicating that you were involved in an incident of relationship violence. This destructive behavior has damaged other people close to you (emotionally and/or physically)—and it has been damaging to you as well. Even though your partner or other people in your life may have acted destructively as well, our focus in this program is on the one person over whom you have control: yourself.

This program will help you discover how abusive patterns in your most intimate relationships began—and it will help you develop new ways of dealing with the beliefs and emotions that have triggered these behaviors.

The same relationship issues can emerge in straight and LGBTQ+ relationships—and the STOP Program for Women group leaders are trained to understand and help with all types of intimate partner relationships. Many of the handouts use examples of situations for female same-sex couples.

The STOP Program for Women should really be called the "GO Program"—because it is designed to move forward with something better and new, not just stop the destructive and old.

Some of the issues are difficult to face, but the STOP Program for Women will help you deal with these problems in a supportive learning environment.

The STOP Program for Women offers women (just like the men in men's groups) intensive training in new skills for self-management, communication, problem solving, and empathy for others. Special attention is paid to the self-talk that determine emotions and behaviors in any given situation.

And this program especially helps women examine the ways they have been victimized in their personal lives—WITHOUT allowing these victim experiences to be used as an excuse for aggressive or abusive behavior.

But, most importantly, the STOP Program for Women group leaders consistently use an approach that emphasizes respect for women's experiences—both in personal history and in present relationships. The group leaders will always try to be compassionate and understanding about why you choose to act the way you do.

In a series of weekly groups, you and the other women in your group will have a chance to discuss family problems, feelings that led to destructive behaviors, and the impact violence has had on your relationships. We strongly emphasize new ways of communicating, handling stress, and resolving conflicts. Each session is designed to focus on a particular aspect of family violence. At each session your group leaders will assign exercises, handouts, and homework, which are included here.

This model has been carefully constructed through decades of trial and error with thousands of women and through paying attention to new research in the field. We would like to thank all the women who have given so much of themselves and worked so hard throughout the years during which we have been developing the program. We have found that domestic violence has many causes and consequences and that each man and woman has a unique story to tell.

Although many of the group sessions involve learning specific skills such as stress management and improved communication, the groups are considered to be group counseling. This means that we encourage you to think about your own life, discuss your feelings, and offer support for other group members. You will get from this program what you put into it. Use your time well.

THE STOP PROGRAM FOR WOMEN Q&A

Welcome to the STOP Program for Women. The following is a list of answers to frequently asked questions about the groups. Please read this information carefully.

1. ***Why was I referred to the STOP Program for Women?***
   You were referred to this program because of reports that you were involved in one or more incidents of relationship violence. The fact that you have been referred to the STOP Program for Women indicates that this problem is treatable.

2. ***How often do the groups meet?***
   Each group meets for two hours, once each week.

3. ***Who else is in the group?***
   The group members include women like yourself who have been involved in some sort of relationship violence. This is an ongoing group. It is very valuable to have group members at different stages of treatment to help explain to you how the group works. The group may include women in both straight and gay relationships.

4. ***What happens in the group?***
   Our philosophy is that women who get into trouble in their relationships need to learn new skills. We want to make sure that you have new ways of handling stress, new ways of thinking about difficult relationship situations, and new ways of problem solving. When you leave this program, you should have lots of new tools to help you handle things differently. This will make it much less likely that the same problems will take place.

   Each session is designed to focus on a particular aspect of relationship health and/or relationship violence. Groups provide an atmosphere to discuss the problems, feelings that have led to destructive behavior, and the impact violence has had on the relationship. New ways of understanding yourself, understanding others, and relating to other people are strongly emphasized.

5. ***Is this a class or group counseling?***
   Although many of the group sessions may involve teaching of specific skills, such as stress management and improved communication, the groups are considered to be group counseling. This means that a strong emphasis is placed on self-examination,

discussion of feelings, and support for other group members. Most people benefit from the group based on how committed they are to engage in these tasks.

6. ***Do I have to come every week?***
   You are required to attend every week. Research indicates that there is a direct relationship between steady attendance and treatment progress. In order for you to benefit from the program, attendance must become a priority. As you become more involved in the group, you will probably find out that you are motivated to attend, not only for your own benefit, but also to support your fellow group members.

7. ***What about absences?***
   We recognize that there may be circumstances which require you to miss a group session. If you are unable to attend a group session, please notify our staff beforehand to let us know that you will be unable to attend. Documentation of all absences is required and should be given to our staff prior to your absence. If you miss a group for unexpected reasons, please bring in documentation for the absence at the next group session. Undocumented absences will be considered unexcused.

   Unexcused absences indicate a lack of interest or commitment to change your situation. An unexcused absence will be grounds for a report back to your probation officer or other referring agency, which may result in the termination of treatment.

8. ***What happens if I arrive late?***
   If a group member arrives more than five minutes late, she will be marked as late. Three times late will be treated as the equivalent of one unexcused absence. If a group member arrives 15 or more minutes late, she will under no circumstances be allowed into the group, and this will be considered an unexcused absence.

9. ***Who leads the group?***
   All of the group leaders are certified domestic violence counselors who have had extensive training in the treatment of relationship violence.

10. ***Are there additional expectations for successful participation other than group attendance?***
    All sessions have homework assignments that you will be expected to complete and bring to the next group meeting. The group leaders will review the homework assignment with you at the end of each group meeting so you will know what is expected. The group leaders will also discuss the completed homework at the beginning of each group meeting. Three missed homework assignments will be considered the equivalent of one unexcused absence. This will be grounds for a report back to your probation officer, case manager, social worker, or other referring agency, which may result in the termination of treatment.

    Group members are required to be at the site 10 minutes before the starting time for the group in order to fill out a questionnaire titled "Weekly Check-In." Group will not begin until everyone completes the questionnaire.

    You will be given a STOP Program for Women: Homework and Handouts binder at the first group meeting. Each week, information from the binder will be discussed during the group session. You are expected to bring your binder to each group meeting.

11. ***What about confidentiality? Can what I say in the group be used against me?***
Since this treatment uses a team approach, you can assume that what you say in the group may be discussed with your probation officer, case manager, social worker, or other referring agency. Only information that is directly related to your treatment goals is included in these reports. Most of the personal issues and feelings discussed in the group sessions remain confidential.

    In certain situations, the group leaders are obligated to report information that is revealed in the group. These reportable situations include serious threats of hurting or killing someone else, serious threats of hurting or killing yourself, new and significant reports of family violence (including incidents in which children have suffered emotional damage from witnessing spousal abuse), child abuse, or elder abuse.

12. ***What about new incidents of violence in my relationship?***
As a participant in domestic violence treatment, you are expected to discuss any new incidents of violence in your relationships. Presenting information about new incidents of violence does not necessarily lead to termination if you are genuinely remorseful, take responsibility for your actions, and appear to be making efforts to prevent a similar reoccurrence in the future. Keep in mind that it is in your best interest to disclose a new incident of violence. When these incidents are discovered through other sources, it impacts negatively on you.

13. ***What about electronic devices?***
During the group session, please turn off all electronic devices. You will have an opportunity during the break to return phone messages.

14. ***How should I dress for the group?***
There is no specific dress code for these sessions.

15. ***Any other rules about appropriate behavior?***
While on the premises of this agency, you are asked to use respectful language that is not offensive to staff or other clients being served.

    No use of alcohol or illegal drugs prior to the group session.

    Group members will not threaten or intimidate other group members or leaders at any time.

    I have read the above information and agree to the conditions of treatment.

_______________________________	_______________________________
Group Member's Signature	Print Name
_______________________________	_______________________________
Date	Group Name

TYPICAL QUESTIONS AND CONCERNS

1. ***Won't group counseling try and get me to let out all my emotions? I'm not comfortable with that!***
   Everybody in group counseling is different, and each person decides how much of her personal emotions and personal experiences to reveal to others. No one is expected to walk right in and talk about their deepest feelings in front of a bunch of strangers.

   Over time, most people become more and more comfortable letting the group know more about what is happening inside. We know that there is usually a correlation between talking about yourself and getting some benefit from the sessions. But this all happens at the pace of the individual.

2. ***I would rather have individual counseling because I don't like talking in front of other people and I can get more personal attention.***
   The STOP Program philosophy is that these kinds of problems are best treated in a group setting. You get the benefit of hearing about the experiences of others and learning from their successes and mistakes. The feedback from peers is one of the single most important factors in predicting positive outcome.

3. ***I don't want to be in a group with a bunch of violent and abusive women—I'm not like them!***
   We treat the woman, not the label. We stay away from labels that sound like put-downs. Instead, we focus on the specific thoughts, feelings, and situations that have led to problem behaviors. We could put any woman in this group, regardless of what has gone wrong in her behavior with others, and she would benefit from the approaches used in this treatment model.

PROVISIONAL STATUS POLICY (GROUP MEMBERS' VERSION)

The following are grounds for group members to be placed on Provisional Status in the STOP Program for Women (leading to possible termination). These behaviors are in addition to activity that takes place outside of the group sessions, such as acts of violence, repeated drug or alcohol problems, or failure to attend group:

1. **Consistently** putting down men or minimizing violence
2. **Persistent** disruptive or oppositional behavior in group
3. **Consistent** projection of blame for relationship problems without self-examination
4. **Consistent** lack of participation in group, including failure to complete homework assignments
5. **Consistent** pattern of telling stories (bragging or showing off) about controlling, abusive, or violent behavior with little or no signs of remorse

THE FIFTEEN COMMANDMENTS OF STOP

1. We are all 100% responsible for our own actions. Even when it *feels* like someone else made us do it.
2. Violence is not an acceptable solution to problems.
3. Anger is normal. Being consumed by anger, or being driven to commit acts of aggression or retaliation because of anger, is not.
4. Recognize that anger is—always—a secondary emotion. Identify the primary one first, and you are really in a position of power.
5. We do not have control over any other person, but we do have control over ourselves.
6. We can always take a time-out before reacting.
7. We can't do anything about the past, but we can change the future.
8. Self-talk is everything. We are always telling ourselves stories about the events in our world—and the stories can always change.
9. Sometimes anger can be very quiet and cold. Just because you are not yelling—or even if you are smiling—does not mean that you are not being aggressive.
10. Just because it feels like someone deserves retaliation doesn't mean it is wise, productive, or moral to deliver it.
11. When you let go of anger, you are doing yourself a big favor. You are no longer allowing the situation or the person to control you.
12. Use gratitudes when you need to, and appreciate the power and positivity they will confer on you.
13. Always have a Prevention Plan in your back pocket. And think of the big picture (the "other three squares").
14. Although there are differences between men and women, our needs and rights are fundamentally alike.
15. Counselors and case managers cannot make people change—they can only set the stage for change to occur.

GRATITUDE STATEMENTS

- Does gratitude really affect your brain at the biological level? YES!
- The antidepressant Wellbutrin boosts the neurotransmitter called dopamine. So does gratitude.
- Prozac boosts the neurotransmitter called *serotonin*. So does gratitude.
- It's not finding gratitude that matters most; it's remembering to look in the first place. Remembering to be grateful is a form of emotional intelligence.
- And gratitude doesn't just make your brain happy—it can also create a positive feedback loop in your relationships. So express that gratitude to the people you care about.

It's not happiness that brings us gratitude. It's gratitude that bring us happiness.

People who kept a list of a few things they were grateful for each day . . .

- exercise more/feel more energy and vitality
- are less bothered by pain
- sleep 30 minutes more each night
- feel closer and more connected to others
- report greater well-being and optimism
- report more attentiveness, enthusiasm, and determination
- cope better with situations that might have made them angry

For example, it can be very valuable to think of one person who has been very important to you, and write down the three most important things that this person has done for you.

At the beginning of each session, we will ask you to share some "good stuff" that you have noticed since we last met. Here are examples of things that might happen in your life in a typical week that are worthy of gratitude:

- *I had a great conversation with my partner last night—I used what we learned in the group, and he said it was one of the best conversations we ever had. I am so grateful.*
- *I talked to a friend of mine and helped her out with a problem. I am grateful that I got a chance to do that.*
- *Somebody at work here really took one of my concerns seriously and followed through on it. I am really grateful.*
- *I watched my kids playing together last night and they were really getting along. I really felt lucky.*

ONE-MINUTE MINDFULNESS IN EVERYDAY LIFE

Mindfulness is a form of self-awareness training: a state of being *in the present* and *accepting things for what they are* (non-judgmentally).

In practice, we want you to just observe whatever happens. Label any thoughts (*oh, there goes a "worried" thought*) and then leave them alone—just be prepared to let them float away. Pay attention to your breathing or simply notice your surroundings instead.

When emotions or memories show up, just give them labels like *that's a sad feeling* or *that's an angry feeling*—and then just allow them to drift away. These memories and feelings will gradually decrease in intensity and frequency.

It is especially helpful to know that you can get a LOT of benefit from mindfulness even if you just practice it for one minute—especially if you can do it several times a day. This is not hard to do, because there is always a minute here or a minute there when you are standing in line, waiting on a phone hold, or just about to walk in the door at home.

One-Minute Mindfulness Technique

In our group, we practice ONE-MINUTE MINDFULNESS every session. Start by sitting in a comfortable and balanced position. Then breathe slowly and deeply several times. Then . . .

- Focus your entire attention on holding a pen or pencil between your fingers for one minute.
- Chew on a raisin for one minute, paying full attention to the taste and texture of this experience.
- Walk three feet (and no more), taking a full minute to take the steps, focusing on all the sensations and feelings in your body as you move so slowly.
- Pick a spot on the wall across from you and focus all of your attention on that spot for one minute.
- Invent your own!

You may be pleasantly surprised to discover what a difference these minutes make. And you can do this anywhere.

FEELINGS COUNT

Handout (page 16 in *Handouts & Homework*)

Happy And Confident

Accepted	Alive	Brave	Calm	Caring	Cheerful
Comfortable	Confident	Excited	Friendly	Fulfilled	Generous
Grateful	Happy	Hopeful	Joyful	Lovable	Loving
Peaceful	Playful	Powerful	Proud	Relaxed	Relieved
Respected	Secure	Understood	Valuable	Warm	Worthwhile

Fearful and Worried

Anxious	Apprehensive	Confused	Desperate	Distrustful
Fearful	Helpless	Horrified	Inhibited	Out of Control
Trapped	Panicky	Pressured	Threatened	Overwhelmed
Troubled	Uncertain	Uneasy	Uptight	Vulnerable
Worried				

Angry And Resentful

Angry	Bitter	Contemptuous	Disgusted	Disrespected
Frustrated	Furious	Hostile	Impatient	Irritated
Outraged	Provoked	Resentful	Stubborn	Unappreciated
Used	Victimized			

Sad And Pessimistic

Confused	Defeated	Depressed	Devastated	Disappointed
Discouraged	Helpless	Hopeless	Isolated	Lonely
Miserable	Trapped	Sad	Stuck	Overwhelmed
Useless				

Uncomfortable And Insecure

Awkward	Embarrassed	Foolish	Humiliated	Inhibited
Insecure	Self-conscious	Shy	Uncomfortable	

Apologetic And Guilty

Apologetic	Guilty	Remorseful	Sorry	Untrustworthy

Hurt And Rejected

Devastated Excluded Hurt Ignored Rejected
Vulnerable

Jealous And Left Out

Envious Deprived Left out Jealous

Ashamed And Inadequate

Ashamed Inferior Inadequate Incompetent Stupid
Useless Unattractive Unworthy Powerless

PART IV

NEW MEMBER SESSIONS

NEW MEMBER SESSION I
House of Abuse

THIS MATERIAL (OR THE MATERIAL FROM NEW MEMBER SESSION II) SHOULD BE PRESENTED ONLY WHEN ONE OR MORE GROUP MEMBERS IS BEGINNING THE PROGRAM. THEN THE REGULARLY SCHEDULED GROUP CONTENT SHOULD RESUME.

NEW MEMBER SESSION I AND NEW MEMBER SESSION II SHOULD EACH BE PRESENTED ON ALTERNATE MONTHS.

Materials:

House of Abuse

Program:

1. In this session, all group members should split up into dyads, interviewing each other *only* about basic information. This *not* the time to ask about or report information about the offense that led to their assignment to this program: *Please pair up with one of the group members next to you. You will have a few minutes each to get some basic information from your partner: What is her name? Is she currently married or together with her partner? What is her name? Does she have kids? What are their names and ages? Where is she from? What kind of work does she do? What are her interests and hobbies? What do you expect to get out of this group? What do you think you can add to the group? You don't need to find out any details about how they ended up here in the group. We save that for much later. Then you will introduce your partner to the group.* At the end of this, and throughout the early group sessions, group leaders should seek out ways to establish connections among group members, such as those who are parents, those who are from similar parts of the country, and so on.

Each partner then reports back to the group at large, introducing her partner to the rest of the group. Even if many of the women have already been through this exercise previously, they should still pair up with a new partner and go through it again.

Remember that, because of intermittent attendance, many of the group members may be new to each other even if this is not their own first session.

It is usually best to keep personal abuse and violence information to a minimum in the first session for a new group member.

2. Begin explaining the basic concept of the House of Abuse by drawing a diagram of the House of Abuse on the board. By the end of this program, the following categories will be listed in the different rooms:

- Physical
- Verbal/Emotional/Psychological
- Social Isolation
- Gender Privilege
- Intimidation
- Sexual
- Child Abuse

3. It is also important to repeatedly emphasize the 100% Rule. This rule states that we are each 100% responsible for our own behavior. Being angry or hurt does not have to lead to abuse or intimidation.

It has proven very valuable in this exercise to develop descriptions that are as gender-neutral as possible. Most of these forms of destructive conflicts can just as easily be used by a woman against a man as the other way around, with the obvious exceptions of, for the most part, sexual abuse. The goal here is to open up valuable discussion and to help the group members discuss these issues without feeling defensive.

4. Begin by asking for a definition of the most obvious kinds of destructive conflict, or abusive behavior, from one person in a relationship toward another—this will usually involve physical abuse and probably yelling and screaming. Ask the question: *What are some ways that someone in an intimate adult relationship could be destructive or abusive to his or her partner? How can somebody abuse another?* As the group identifies different themes, label the different rooms, and fill in some of the examples in the room where they best fit. Here are some basic descriptions of what belongs in each room:

a. **Physical.** This is the easiest to identify. This includes any kind of aggressive physical contact, including hitting, choking, pushing, and so on. Make sure to review every possible form that the group can generate. The group members usually describe this first.

b. **Verbal/Emotional/Psychological.** This is also easy to identify. This includes any kind of name-calling, verbal put-downs, criticism, and so on. This also involves the use of mind games. When a man or woman teases his or her partner about their weight or body and then protests that they were only kidding or only asking a question, they are committing psychological abuse. When she humiliates him in public, she is doing the same thing. Often, men drill home the message that "you could never make it without me." When people hear this enough times, they may begin to believe it. Humiliating someone for not being successful or competent at something is psychological abuse. Another form of destructive conflict in this category is ignoring someone: the silent treatment. This can be one of the most powerful mind games of all, wearing someone down until they desperately try to "be good."

c. **Intimidation.** This includes threats to kill or hurt the other person, threats against the kids, or threats of kidnapping the kids. It may involve telling him or her that a judge will never give her custody because she's crazy or doesn't work or has used drugs in the past. Threatening suicide is another example of intimidation—this can be a very powerful way of controlling someone because they are desperate to avoid the terrible guilt and pain. The goal of these gambits is to produce FEAR, which is used to maintain dominance and control.

d. **Sexual.** The most blatant form of sexual abuse is rape. However, this is not the only form of sexual abuse in a relationship. Demanding that the partner watch or read pornography can be abusive. Insisting on certain sex acts that he or she finds humiliating or degrading can be abusive.

e. **Social Isolation.** This category is often overlooked. This is more typical male-to-female, but could work the other way around. Because they feel threatened, people may become determined to prevent their partner from becoming independent or successful. This may involve sabotaging the partner's attempts to work, go to school, or have friends or activities of their own. The fear is that the partner won't need him or her anymore if the partner develops in this way. This is the ultimate indication of insecurity.

f. **Gender Privilege.** The male gender privilege form of destructive conflicts includes the entitlement men claim that leads them to dominate the relationship. The man who insists on using the fact that he is the breadwinner to demand that he make decisions for the marriage and family would be an example. This same attitude can be used to demand sex, get out of household chores, or demand more control over his free time than his wife or partner is allowed. A man may tell his wife or partner that he "needs" to go away with his buddies for a week; what would it be like if she told him the same thing, and if she just assumed that he would watch the kids and take care of the business at home?

The female gender privilege form of destructive conflicts includes the female's insistence that she have more control over child-rearing decisions or the color of the new sofa. If a woman insists that she shouldn't have to work because *that's the man's job*, we have an example of female gender privilege. Or, if she feels like it's OK to hit her male partner because she's female, but it's not OK for him to hit her.

g. **Child Abuse.** Any physical, sexual, verbal, or emotional form of child abuse is likewise a destructive conflict in the marriage. Using the kids as pawns in the battle between parents or threatening to hurt the kids would be examples here also. This can often lead to a discussion about the ways in which abused children often become abusers themselves in the next generation.

After establishing the rooms of the House of Abuse, ask the group members to consider the following questions:

Is this a house that you would like to live in?

You don't have to say anything out loud, but see if you recognize any of these rooms as rooms in your house right now.

Again, don't say anything out loud, but see if you recognize any of these rooms as rooms in the house you grew up in.

Would you say that most of the examples we have come up with are illegal or criminal behavior? If not, then be aware that we are defining abusive behavior in relationships as anything that is clearly hurtful or destructive in this relationship—even if you can't go to jail for it.

THE HOUSE OF ABUSE

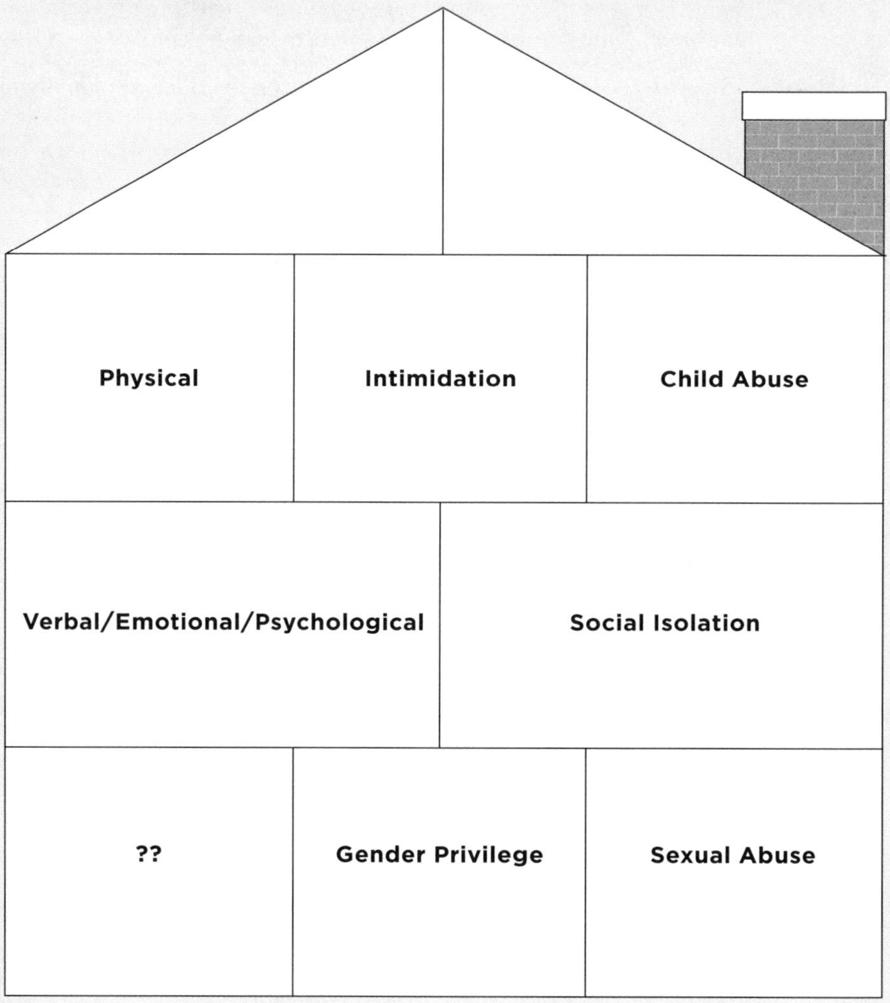

Adapted with permission from Fischer, K. L., & McGrane, M. F. (1997). *Journey beyond abuse: A step-by-step guide to facilitating women's domestic abuse groups.* St Paul: Amherst H. Wilder Foundation.

TO FOCUS ON ALCOHOL AND DRUG ISSUES . . .

1. Add a room for substance abuse to the House of Abuse.

NEW MEMBER SESSION II

Time-Out

Materials:

Time-Out
Time-Out Information for Partners

Program:

1. In this session, all group members should split up into dyads, interviewing each other *only* about basic information. This *not* the time to ask about or report information about the offense that led to their assignment to this program. *Please pair up with one of the group members next to you. You will have a few minutes each to get some basic information from your partner: What is her name? Is she currently married or together with her partner? What is her name? Does she have kids? What are their names and ages? Where is she from? What kind of work does she do? What are her interests and hobbies? What do you expect to get out of this group? What do you think you can add to the group? You don't need to find out any details about how they ended up here in the group. We save that for much later. Then you will introduce your partner to the group.* At the end of this, and throughout the early group sessions, group leaders should seek out ways to establish connections among group members, such as those who are parents, those who are from similar parts of the country, and so on.

   Each partner then reports back to the group at large, introducing her partner to the rest of the group. Even if many of the women have already been through this exercise previously, they should still pair up with a new partner and go through it again.

   Remember that, because of intermittent attendance, many of the group members may be new to each other even if this is not their own first session.

   It is usually best to keep personal abuse and violence information to a minimum in the first session for a new group member.

2. TIME-OUT
   a. Introduce the idea of having a plan for episodes when it feels like behavior is getting out of control. This requires personal responsibility—to recognize the signals and to act responsibly in those situations. The odds of being successful with this plan are much higher when people have thought about it, planned for it, and rehearsed it in advance.

b. Review Time-Out: The technique does not help the couple resolve the issue at hand; thus, it is a stopgap measure. However, it often prevents violence, which is the primary goal. Communication skills can be learned later, after the fear of any destructive behavior (verbal or physical abuse) is gone.

Model the use of the skill with a coleader or one of the group members.

Make sure that the group members inform their partners—in advance—of the purpose and steps involved with the time-out.

c. Review Time-Out Information for Partners. Be prepared for the group discussion in which the group members protest that their partners will never put up with a time-out. It is important to empathize with this concern because, in many cases, it is legitimate. Emphasize that we are offering approaches which are not guaranteed to work, but which simply decrease the probability of an explosion.

TO FOCUS ON ALCOHOL AND DRUG ISSUES . . .

1. Review how much more difficult it is to effectively implement a time-out if one or both partners have been drinking or using.
2. Emphasize the extreme importance of not drinking or using during a time-out.

TIME-OUT

Handout (page 19 in *Handouts & Homework*)

The time-out is an emergency strategy to prevent dangerous escalation of conflicts. It should *only* be used in crisis—and as you learn better communication and self-management skills, it may never have to be used at all. But you must know how to use it effectively.

IF YOU USE A TIME-OUT FREQUENTLY, SOMETHING IS SERIOUSLY WRONG WITH YOUR RELATIONSHIP. DO NOT USE TIME-OUT SIMPLY BECAUSE YOU WISH TO AVOID TALKING ABOUT A CERTAIN SUBJECT. THIS IS FOR EMERGENCIES ONLY, AND YOU MUST BE PREPARED TO RESUME THE DISCUSSION LATER ON.

Time-out should not be used as a weapon against the other person. It should not be used as a way of avoiding conflicts. It should not be used as a way of making the other person feel abandoned (*"I'm outta here, dude—I'll show you who's in charge!"*).

Instead, time-out should be used as a sign of respect for the relationship. The message is this: *I care enough about us that I don't want any more damage to this relationship.* It is essential that your partner understand this message of respect. It is your job to clearly explain this in advance—and to follow it up by your actions when using the time-out correctly.

1. *I'm beginning to feel like things are getting out of control.*
2. *And I don't want to do anything that would mess up our relationship.*
3. *So I need to take a time-out.*
4. *I'm going out for a walk around the neighborhood (or my sister's house, or the gym, etc.).*
5. *I'll be back in (five minutes, or one hour, etc.).*
6. *And let's try talking about this again when I get back. Okay?*

Partner responds:

7. *Okay. Time-out.*

If he or she does not acknowledge, begin the time-out anyway—*without* making any physical contact or threats!

- Leave silently—no door slamming.
- While away, don't drink or use drugs—and don't drive if your temper is out of control.
- Try using self-talk that will help you keep this in perspective:
  - I'm getting upset, but I don't have to lose my cool!
  - I'm frustrated, but I don't have to control anybody else or always get my way.
  - I can calm myself and think through this situation.
  - I've got to think about what will be most important for the future.

- Do something physical (walking, playing sports, working out, etc.) if it will help you discharge tension. Try distracting yourself with any activity that temporarily takes your mind off the intensity of the argument.
- **You must come back when you said you would, or call and check in.** When you come back, decide together if you want to continue the discussion. Here are the options at this point:
  - **Discuss it now:** This is usually the best and most respectful action, but there are some exceptions.
  - **Drop the issue:** Maybe you both realize now that it was really not that big a deal.
  - **Put the issue on hold:** This may be important to discuss, but it would be better to do it at later time. As long as *both* parties agree, this can work.
- Each person has the right to say *no* to further discussion at that time and to suggest a time for discussion. If anger escalates again, take another time-out.

TIME-OUT INFORMATION FOR PARTNERS

Handout (page 21 in *Handouts & Homework*)

1. **How do time-outs help solve our family problems?**
Your partner's use of time-outs will prevent both of you from escalating into physical or psychological abuse. Time-outs alone do not solve destructive conflicts, but if used faithfully they will help you both avoid extremely destructive behavior. No respectful communication takes place when there is abuse. Time-outs should be used in an emergency to prevent irreparable damage to the relationship.

2. **What do I do if every time I want to discuss an important topic with my partner, she says she is taking a time-out?**
Let your partner take the time-out anyway. If she becomes angry and abusive, you will not be able to talk about the problems. At first, she may take time-outs a lot. Just remind yourself that it is only one step and that she will be using other approaches as well.

3. **What if my partner refuses to discuss the matter even after the time-out?**
Notice on the instruction sheet that she has several choices as to what she does after a time-out. She is not supposed to drop issues if they are important to you. However, she may put them on hold until she is able to both calmly speak and *listen to you*. If she refuses to discuss an issue, your insisting will *not* bring about communication. Let her know that you are still interested in talking about the issue, but be willing to set a later time when she can be calmer while discussing it.

4. **Should I remind my partner to take a time-out when she is getting angry or abusive?**
No. She is responsible for identifying her own feelings and taking the time-out. As long as you do it for her, she is *not* doing her job. If you are upset about her abuse, you take a time-out for yourself as long as you can do it safely. Remember, you cannot control another person's behavior; you can only protect yourself.

5. **What should I do when she takes a time-out during a discussion?**
Remind yourself that this is the first step—that it is better for her to take a time-out than to be abusive toward you. Waiting for her to return can lead to your feeling frustrated or abandoned. You can use the time for yourself and then go about your regular business.

6. **Would time-outs be useful for me?**
Yes. If you find your own anger rising, a time-out is a tool you can use to calm down before you go further in working out a conflict. However, your time-outs will not necessarily change your partner's behaviors.

PART V

PROGRAM SESSIONS: ANGER AND AGGRESSION

Session 1

THE RED FLAGS OF ANGER

Materials:

Female Abuse Wheel
Red Flags of Anger
Video: *When Women Abuse Men* (https://www.youtube.com/watch?v=gZVJoSP4UEU&feature=youtu.be)
Anger Styles Quiz
What's Your Anger Style?

Program:

1. Ask each group member to report one gratitude (p. 59).
2. Focus on the mindfulness exercise (p. 60) for one minute.
3. Review the homework from the previous week.
4. Review the Weekly Check-Ins and use these to help guide the group discussion.
5. Review the Female Abuse Wheel. Help the group members identify examples of their own behavior toward their partners which belong on this wheel. Be prepared for resistance and rationalization. Remember to focus on how the choice of behavior is separate from feeling justified.
6. Introduce the concept of red flags. Go over the handout "The Red Flags of Anger" and get examples from each group member in each category. Explain how important it is to identify the warning signs of anger. Remind the group members that the more they know about themselves, the more true power they have over their own behavior. Refer to Commandment 5.

TO FOCUS ON ALCOHOL AND DRUG ISSUES . . .

1. When discussing the red flags of anger, make sure to identify any drinking or using as one kind of red flag.
2. Discuss how alcohol and other substances are likely to make each of the anger styles more severe.
3. Discuss how much more frequently people engage in emotional abuse when they are in an altered state, because substances affect both perception and judgment.

FEMALE ABUSE WHEEL

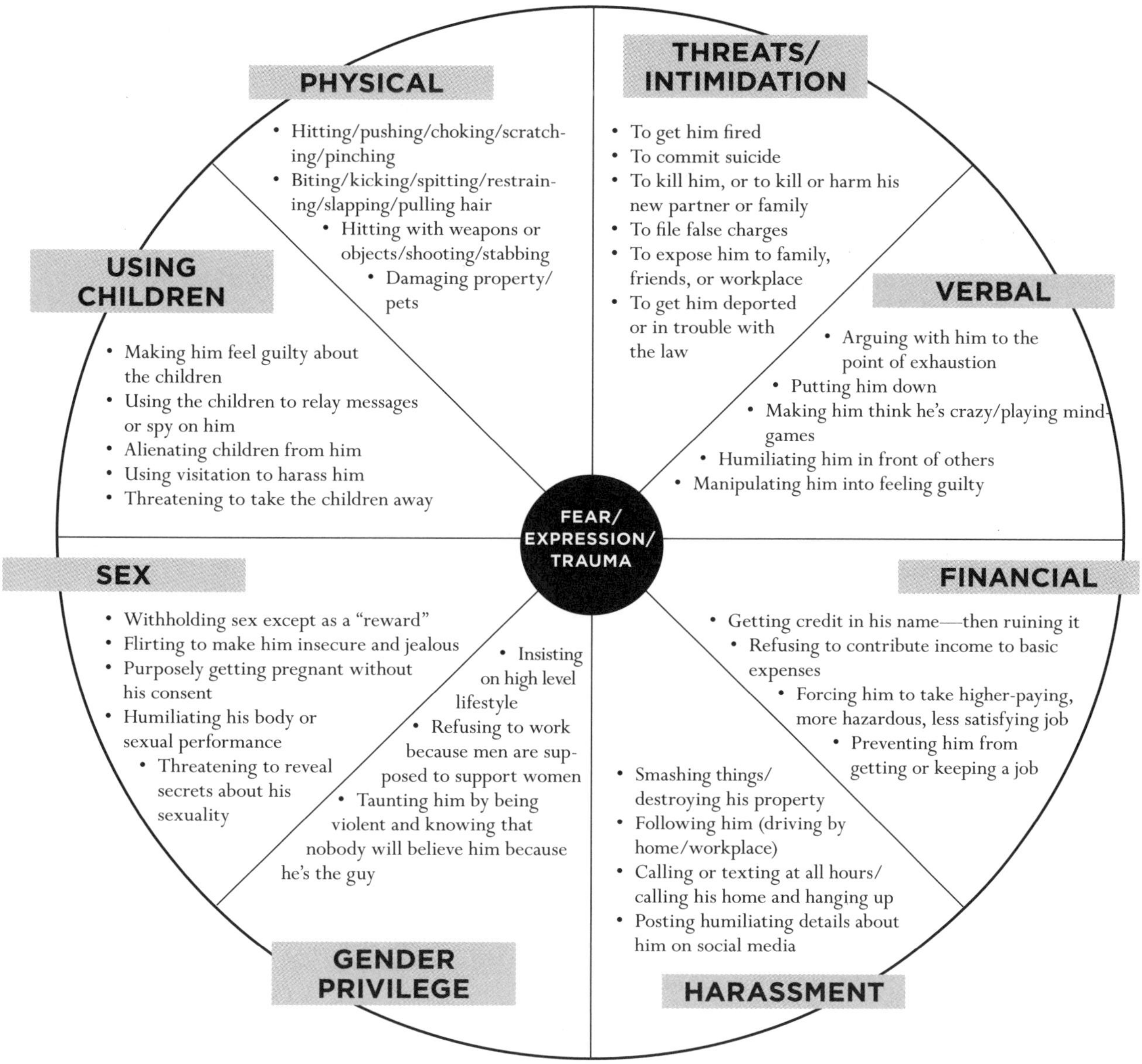

Adapted with permission from "Female Aggression Wheel," created by Araceli Cabarcas in Koonin, M., Cabarcas, A., & Geffner, R. (2002). Women Ending Abusive/Violent Episodes Respectfully (WEAVER) Manual. San Diego CA: Family Violence and Sexual Assault Institute.

RED FLAGS OF ANGER

Handout **(page 23 in *Handouts & Homework*)**

Red flags are warnings. They tell us that we are entering an emotional state, a way of thinking, or a situation where we may feel really angry, lose control, and/or escalate. Becoming aware of these red flag signals helps us remain in control of ourselves and behaviors.

Physical Red Flags

What physical cues (cues in your body) will tell you that you are getting really angry and beginning to escalate?

- Muscle tension
- Heartbeat
- Disorientation

Self-Talk Red Flags

What kind of self-talk do you begin to have when your anger is rising and you are beginning to escalate?

- *He's trying to make a fool of me.*
- *He doesn't love me anymore.*
- *I think he wants to leave me.*
- *Are you* seriously *expecting me to do that for you?*
- *Somebody needs to teach him a lesson!*

Situational Red Flags

- Paying bills
- Hearing certain questions
- Dealing with kids
- After having a few drinks

What are the situations that are almost sure to start an argument between you and your partner?

When you know what these are, you can plan a whole lot better—either by avoiding some of them, or by being extra careful to monitor your own behavior.

SESSION 1 HOMEWORK #1

Handout (page 24 in *Handouts & Homework*)

Identify three examples from the Female Abuse Wheel that you have engaged in with your partner. Be specific:

1.

2.

3.

SESSION 1 HOMEWORK #2

Handout (page 25 in *Handouts & Homework*)

Fill this out in preparation for the next session:

ANGER STYLES QUIZ

1.	I try never to get angry.	YES	NO
2.	I get really nervous when others are angry.	YES	NO
3.	I feel I'm doing something bad when I get angry.	YES	NO
4.	I often tell people I'll do what they want, but then I forget.	YES	NO
5.	I frequently say things like "Yeah, but . . . " and "I'll do it later."	YES	NO
6.	People tell me I must be angry but I'm not sure why.	YES	NO
7.	I get mad at myself a lot.	YES	NO
8.	I "stuff" my anger and then get headaches, stomachaches, etc.	YES	NO
9.	I frequently call myself ugly names like "dummy, selfish, etc."	YES	NO
10.	My anger comes on really fast.	YES	NO
11.	I act before I think when I get angry.	YES	NO
12.	My anger goes away very quickly.	YES	NO
13.	I get very angry when people criticize me.	YES	NO
14.	People say I am easily hurt and oversensitive.	YES	NO
15.	I get angry easily when I feel bad about myself.	YES	NO
16.	I get mad in order to get what I want.	YES	NO
17.	I try to scare others with my anger.	YES	NO
18.	I sometimes pretend to be mad when I'm not really angry.	YES	NO
19.	Sometimes I get angry just for the excitement or action.	YES	NO
20.	I like the strong feelings that come with my anger.	YES	NO
21.	Sometimes when I am bored I start arguments or pick fights.	YES	NO
22.	I seem to get angry all the time.	YES	NO
23.	My anger feels like a bad habit I have trouble breaking.	YES	NO
24.	I get mad without thinking—it feels automatic.	YES	NO
25.	I get jealous a lot, even when there is no reason.	YES	NO
26.	I don't trust people very much.	YES	NO
27.	Sometimes it feels like people are out to get me.	YES	NO

28.	I become very angry when I defend my beliefs and opinions.	YES	NO
29.	I often feel outraged about what others try to get away with.	YES	NO
30.	I always know I'm right in an argument.	YES	NO
31.	I hang onto my anger for a long time.	YES	NO
32.	I have a hard time forgiving people.	YES	NO
33.	I hate people for what they've done to me.	YES	NO

Adapted with permission from Potter-Efron, R., & Potter-Efron, P. (2006). Letting go of anger: The eleven most common anger styles and what to do about them. Oakland, CA: New Harbinger.

Session 2

RED FLAGS OF ANGER #2

Materials:

What's Your Anger Style?
The Four-Square Technique
Healthy Anger/Destructive Anger
Letting Go of Anger

Program:

1. Ask each group member to report one gratitude (p. 59).
2. Focus on the mindfulness exercise (p. 60) for one minute.
3. Review the homework from the previous week.
4. Review the Weekly Check-Ins and use these to help guide the group discussion.
5. Review the Anger Styles Quiz (filled out as homework) and What's Your Anger Style?. Use the group members' profiles to help generate a discussion about the different styles of anger that they use.
6. Review Healthy Anger/Destructive Anger.
7. Review the Four-Square Technique and discuss. This is one of our strategies to prevent damage in a relationship even when there is a lot of temptation to do so. Emphasize how powerful the appeal of the upper left-hand box can be, for drinking or using drugs or spending money recklessly, or exploding with rage. The success of the Four-Square Technique hinges on respecting the power of that box—but still finding even more power in the other three boxes.
8. Review Letting Go of Anger.

TO FOCUS ON ALCOHOL AND DRUG ISSUES . . .

1. Apply the Four-Square Technique to drug and alcohol issues.
2. Discuss how the cycle of abuse is more likely to occur when one or both people are drinking or using.

WHAT'S YOUR ANGER STYLE?

Handout (page 27 in *Handouts & Homework*)

Adapted with permission from Potter-Efron, R., & Potter-Efron, P. (2006). Letting go of anger: The eleven most common anger styles and what to do about them. Oakland, CA: New Harbinger.

I. HIDDEN STYLES. These individuals are partly or mostly unaware/unaccepting of their anger.

A. *ANGER AVOIDANCE:* People who believe anger is bad, scary, or useless. They cannot use anger appropriately in their daily lives.
Treatment Approaches: Assertiveness, separate concepts of selfishness from self-caring, permission to be angry.

B. *SNEAKY ANGER:* Passive-aggressive individuals whose power centers on frustrating others through inaction.
Treatment Approaches: Learn to say *yes* and *no*; focus upon positive goals; work with person's developmental history to seek sources of passivity.

C. *ANGER TURNED INWARD:* These people frequently become angry at themselves, sometimes in self-destructive patterns.
Treatment Approaches: Permission to externalize anger if appropriate; improved self-caring.

II. EXPLOSIVE STYLES. These individuals periodically demonstrate their anger and aggression through dramatic outbursts.

A. *SUDDEN ANGER:* Anger comes out as rapid, usually short-lived, intense bursts.
Treatment Approaches: Slow down the anger, time-outs, gain awareness of buildup stage.

B. *SHAME-BASED ANGER:* Anger reflects perceived attacks upon a person's core self.
Treatment Approaches: Address shame-rage connection, self-esteem imprvement, address shame-blame issues.

C. *DELIBERATE ANGER:* Anger that is purposely displayed in order to intimidate.
Treatment Approaches: Discuss gains and losses of this behavior, empathy training, teach alternative communication skills.

D. *EXCITATORY ANGER:* Individuals seek the intensity of the anger rush.
Treatment Approaches: Commitment to calmness and moderation, new lifestyle, connect to stimulant addiction pattern.

III. CHRONIC STYLES. These people have developed long-term anger patterns that keep them angry, bitter, and resentful.

A. *HABITUAL ANGER:* Automatic thoughts and actions perpetuate nonfunctional anger.
Treatment Approaches: Increased awareness of behavior, focus upon person's choices, practice new behavior.

B. *PARANOIA:* Anger projected onto others and then defended against with defensive anger and aggression.

Treatment Approaches: Owning your anger, ending vigilance and proof-seeking behavior, developing trust.

C. *MORAL ANGER:* Anger is perceived as justified, righteous, for a cause greater than self-interest.
Treatment Approaches: Empathy to de-"devilize" others, emphasis on humanity and equality.

D. *RESENTMENT/HATE:* Others are treated as loathsome and unforgivable.
Treatment Approaches: Forgiveness as a gift to oneself, letting go of the past, resentment prevention.

THE FOUR-SQUARE TECHNIQUE

Handout (page 29 in *Handouts & Homework*)

The Four-Square Technique is especially valuable when you are trying to make a decision about how to act. It might be something of major consequence, like whether to be violent with someone, or more of an everyday experience, like how to express your disappointment or unhappiness with one of your kids.

Every decision you make involves four outcomes to consider:

SHORT TERM/SELF	**LONG TERM/SELF**
SHORT TERM/PARTNER	**LONG TERM/PARTNER**

For example, if you are tempted to get drunk at a party (but your boyfriend often suffers when you do this), your Four-Square might look like this:

SHORT TERM/SELF GREAT!	**LONG TERM/SELF** GUILTY
SHORT TERM/ PARTNER HURTFUL	**LONG TERM/PARTNER** ANGRY/MISTRUSTING

Practically everything that you are tempted to do, like getting angry or aggressive, means that the Short Term/Self square is very appealing—otherwise you wouldn't be so tempted to do it. But, before you act, it is very important to consider the other three squares. *Will this be a good decision for other people? Will this be a good decision for me in the long run?*

If the vote on the Four-Square is 3 to 1 against, or even 2 to 2, it is usually a good idea *not* to go there.

HEALTHY ANGER/DESTRUCTIVE AGGRESSION

Handout (page 30 in *Handouts & Homework*)

Everyone gets mad. Anger can be positive if it helps you stand up for yourself or makes things better.

Anger is healthy when . . .

. . . It doesn't turn into physical or verbal aggression.

. . . You take responsibility for your feelings. ("I'm angry," not "You make me mad.")

. . . It's about issues and not personalities. ("I need you to clean up after yourself," not "You're the most selfish person in the universe.")

. . . It lasts a short time and doesn't grow into resentment or grudges; and you can express your anger without saying or doing things that hurt you or others.

When you're angry, it's not okay to . . .

- Hit people
- Hit things
- Scream
- Push or shove
- Name-call
- Threaten
- Throw things
- Slam doors
- Blame
- Become reckless
- Take it out on others
- Draw others into the problem
- Ask others to choose sides
- Hurt yourself

When you're angry, it IS okay to . . .

- Splash water on your face
- Talk to yourself in the mirror
- Cry
- Walk away
- Write an angry letter and tear it up
- Take a time-out
- Send an I-message to tell the person that you are angry
- Ask the person to stop their behavior
- Talk it over with a friend
- Take a deep breath, and hold it in for as long as you can, then let it out as slowly as you can

LETTING GO OF ANGER

Handout (page 32 in *Handouts & Homework*)

Anger is a part of life. Our wish for you, and for ourselves, is to be able to accept the blessing of anger, to listen to its message, and then let go of it.

DO'S AND DON'TS FOR TREATING OTHERS WITH RESPECT

Do . . .

- Begin each day with a promise to respect others.
- Sit down and talk quietly and listen carefully to what others say.
- Look for things to appreciate in others.
- Give praise out loud for the good you see in others.
- Tell others they are good, good enough, and lovable.
- Tell others they are worthwhile and important to you.
- Speak in a quiet voice even when you disagree.
- Pass up chances to insult, attack, or criticize.
- Let others have responsibility for their lives while you take responsibility for yours.

Don't . . .

- Look for things to criticize.
- Make fun or laugh at others.
- Make faces or roll your eyes.
- Tell others how to run their lives.
- Insult others.
- Ignore others.
- Put people down in front of others.
- Act superior.
- Sneer.
- Tell others they're weird or crazy.
- Say others are bad, not good enough, or unlovable.
- Say others don't belong or you wish they were dead.
- Call others names like *fat, ugly, stupid*, or *worthless*.

SESSION 2 HOMEWORK

Handout (page 33 in *Handouts & Homework*)

Review the handout on Healthy Anger/Destructive Aggression. Think of three items on the list of "When You're Angry, It's Okay To . . . " that have worked for you in the past. Then write down three more of your own that aren't on the list:

1.

2.

3.

PART VI

PROGRAM SESSIONS: PERSONAL HISTORY AND PERSONAL EMPOWERMENT

Session 3

SHAME

Materials:

Video: *I, Tonya* (mother shaming leading to adult domestic violence relationship: 23:43–25:21 + 55:05–57:17 + 44:45–45:45)
Put-Downs From Parents
Forgiving the Self

Program:

1. Ask each group member to report one gratitude (p. 59).
2. Focus on the mindfulness exercise (p. 60) for one minute.
3. Review the homework from the previous week.
4. Review the Weekly Check-Ins and use these to help guide the group discussion.
5. Introduce the video clip from *I, Tonya*. Following the clip, it is very important to process feelings that this clip generates for the participants. Use the following questions as a guideline:
   - *What feelings did you experience viewing this clip?*
   - *What do you think that Tonya was feeling?*
   - *In what ways has Tonya's mother shamed her and cursed her?*
   - *What do you think the connection is between the way Tonya grew up and the relationship choices she made?*
   - *What do you think it would take for Tonya to turn her life around after growing up with that mother and getting involved in such a dysfunctional relationship?*
6. It is important to link feelings of abandonment, anxiety, and shame with abusive behavior. Ask group members how suffering shame as a child may have led to negative self-talk and acts of abuse in their intimate relationships.
7. You may want to use the words "problems in your relationship" as opposed to "abusive behavior"; women tend to see themselves as victims and may try to spin the conversation to be how their partners abuse them. Also—sometimes it helps to use the word *put-down* rather than *shame* or *humiliation*. The word *shame* may lead to defensiveness and denial.

8. After this general discussion, ask the group members to fill out the Put-Downs From Parents questionnaire. **We have discovered that people are much more forthcoming about reporting information on this questionnaire after watching this video.** These scales are not to be scored. They are only intended to help stimulate memories and discussion.
9. Review Forgiving the Self and discuss.

TO FOCUS ON ALCOHOL AND DRUG ISSUES . . .

1. Ask the group members what an alcoholic or drug user is most likely to do right after a scene like they just saw in *I, Tonya*.
2. Discuss how chemical dependency is often based on shame and guilt. In some cases the addict started using in order to offset feelings of shame and guilt, and in almost every case the addict now lives with shame and guilt based on things they did to others.

PUT-DOWNS FROM PARENTS

Handout (page 34 in *Handouts & Homework*)

Adapted with permission from Dutton, D. G. (1998). The abusive personality: Violence and control in intimate relationships. New York: Guilford Press.

Please write in the number listed below (1–4) that best describes how often the experience happened to you with your mother (or stepmother, female guardian, etc.) and father (or stepfather, male guardian, etc.) when you were growing up. If you had more than one mother or father figure, please answer for the persons whom you feel played the most important role in your upbringing.

You might choose to share your responses with the group, but that decision will be *completely* up to you. The more honest you can be as you describe yourself and your history, the more you will be able to benefit from this program.

1	2	3	4
Never Occurred	Occasionally Occurred	Sometimes Occurred	Frequently Occurred

	Father	Mother
1. I think that my parent wished I had been a really different kind of child.	_____	_____
2. As a child, I was physically punished or scolded in the presence of others.	_____	_____
3. I was treated as the scapegoat of the family.	_____	_____
4. I felt my parent thought it was my fault when he/she was unhappy.	_____	_____
5. I think my parent was mean and held grudges towards me.	_____	_____
6. I was punished by my parents without having done anything.	_____	_____
7. My parent criticized me and/or told me how useless I was in front of others.	_____	_____
8. My parent beat me for no reason.	_____	_____
9. My parent would be angry with me without letting me know why.	_____	_____

FORGIVING THE SELF

Handout (page 35 in *Handouts & Homework*)

Guilt is the feeling that lets us know when we have made a mistake or violated our own values—feeling guilty can be a very healthy way of motivating us to change.

Guilt = I made a mistake

Shame is the belief—and the horrible feelings that come with it—that we are fundamentally defective.

Shame = I AM a mistake

SHAME	GUILT
I am a failure.	*I failed to do something.*
Everything I do is wrong.	*I make mistakes sometimes.*
This can never be repaired.	*Forgiveness and amends often lead to healing and repair.*
I have to keep this horrible thing secret.	*If I can find someone to talk to about this, I can learn, recover, and grow.*

You can forgive yourself for your mistakes (and release yourself from shame) when you can . . .

1. Stop the behavior.
2. Acknowledge what you did and that you do not want to do it again.
3. Acknowledge that you hurt yourself and/or others.
4. Make amends to others, when possible and appropriate.
5. Explore alternative behaviors that honor your feelings and are respectful to self and others.
6. Move forward in a manner that honors the wisdom you now have and the life you wish for yourself.

SESSION 3 HOMEWORK

Handout (page 36 in *Handouts & Homework*)

Fill out the Put-Downs from Parents chart again, this time from the perspective of one of your own children. If you do not have children, pick a child you know well and try to fill it out from his or her perspective.

1	2	3	4
Never Occurred	Occasionally Occurred	Sometimes Occurred	Frequently Occurred

	Father	Mother
1. I think that my parent wished I had been a really different kind of child.	______	______
2. As a child, I was physically punished or scolded in the presence of others.	______	______
3. I was treated as the scapegoat of the family.	______	______
4. I felt my parent thought it was my fault when he/she was unhappy.	______	______
5. I think my parent was mean and held grudges towards me.	______	______
6. I was punished by my parents without having done anything.	______	______
7. My parent criticized me and/or told me how useless I was in front of others.	______	______
8. My parent beat me for no reason.	______	______
9. My parent would be angry with me without letting me know why.	______	______

Session 4

WHAT'S YOUR ACE SCORE?

Materials:

ACE Info
What's My ACE Score?
ACE Resilience Questionnaire

Program:

1. Ask each group member to report one gratitude (p. 59).
2. Focus on the mindfulness exercise (p. 60) for one minute.
3. Review the homework from the previous week.
4. Review the Weekly Check-Ins and use these to help guide the group discussion.
5. Review the research that generated the Adverse Childhood Experiences (ACE) study, summarized on the ACE Info handout. The study found that the higher the ACE score, the greater the risk of poor physical health, poor mental health, and negative social consequences later in life.

   The study also found a direct correlation between ACE scores and perpetrating domestic violence—both male and female.

6. Read through the What's My ACE Score? items and discuss briefly, to make sure all group members understand the description of the events so they can answer accurately.

   NOTE TO GROUP MEMBERS:
   Sometimes people take exception to the phrasing of Questions 3 and 6, arguing that sexual assault by anyone of any age is traumatic, and that the death of a parent should be included. If, when taking the survey, you prefer to modify the questions to allow for these factors, go ahead.

7. Take a few minutes for all group members to fill out the questionnaire. Then go through each item and ask each group member to report their score for that item. Encourage discussion about these reports.

8. Remind the group members that a high ACE score does *not* doom a woman or a man to medical problems, psychological problems, or behavioral problems. But it *does* increase risk. Remind them that "knowledge is self-power," and knowing that you are at greater risk for certain problems empowers you to be more on the lookout for signs that things are going wrong.
9. Now take a few minutes for all group members to fill out the ACE Resilience Questionnaire. Then go through each item and ask each group member to report their score for that item. Encourage discussion about these reports.
10. It is also very often helpful for the group members to discuss these scores with their partner—*never* as an excuse for bad behavior, but simply so their partner can have more empathy and intimacy.

TO FOCUS ON ALCOHOL AND DRUG ISSUES . . .

1. Lead a group discussion about why it is that adult drug and alcohol problems are so much more common when someone has a higher ACE score.

ADVERSE CHILDHOOD EXPERIENCES (ACE) INFO

Handout (page 37 in *Handouts & Homework*)

- Adverse Childhood Experiences (ACEs) are very common.
- ACEs are strong predictors of later health risks.
- This combination makes ACEs one of the leading predictors of adult health and social well-being.

1. The original ACE study was conducted on 17,337 participants from the Kaiser health care system between 1995 and 1997.
2. About 67% of individuals reported at least one ACE. If someone had one ACE point, they usually had more: 87% who reported one ACE reported at least one additional ACE.
3. The number of childhood ACEs was strongly associated with adult problems with . . .
   - smoking
   - alcohol and drug abuse
   - sexual promiscuity
   - severe obesity
   - depression
   - heart disease
   - cancer
   - chronic lung disease
   - shortened life span
   - domestic violence
4. Compared to an ACE score of zero, having four ACE points is associated with a sevenfold increase in alcoholism, a doubling of risk of being diagnosed with cancer, and a fourfold increase in emphysema.
5. ACE scores above six are associated with a 30-fold increase in attempted suicide.

ACE Score and the
Risk of *Perpetrating* Domestic Violence

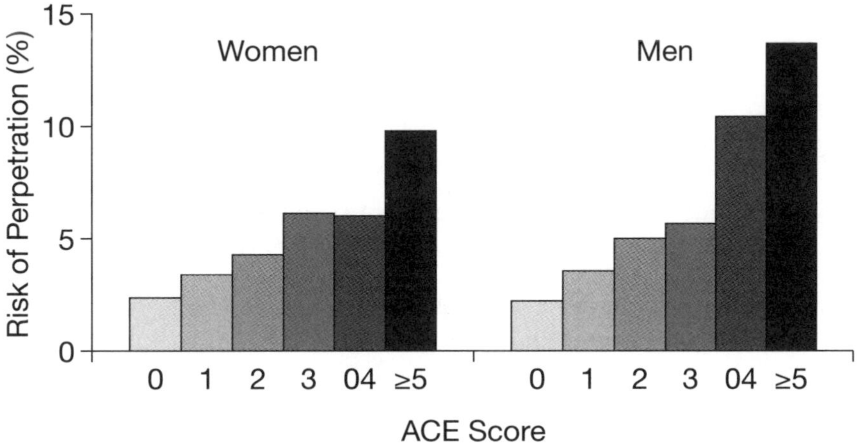

Source: Based on information from Whitfield, C. L., Anda, R. F., Dube, S. R., & Felitti, V. J. (2003). Violent childhood experiences and the risk of intimate partner violence in adults: Assessment in a large health maintenance organization. Journal of Interpersonal Violence, 18(2), 166–185.

WHAT'S MY ACE SCORE?

Handout (page 39 in *Handouts & Homework*)

Prior to your 18th birthday:

1. Did a parent or other adult in the household often or very often . . .
Swear at you, insult you, put you down, or humiliate you?
or
Act in a way that made you afraid that you might be physically hurt?
Yes No If yes, enter 1 ______

2. Did a parent or other adult in the household often or very often . . .
Push, grab, slap, or throw something at you?
or
Ever hit you so hard that you had marks or were injured?
Yes No If yes, enter 1 ______

3. Did an adult or person at least five years older than you ever . . .
Touch or fondle you or have you touch their body in a sexual way?
or
Attempt or actually have oral, anal, or vaginal intercourse with you?
Yes No If yes, enter 1 ______

4. Did you often or very often feel that . . .
No one in your family loved you or thought you were important or special?
or
Your family didn't look out for each other, feel close to each other, or support each other?
Yes No If yes, enter 1 ______

5. Did you often or very often feel that . . .
You didn't have enough to eat, had to wear dirty clothes, and had no one to protect you?
or
Your parents were too drunk or high to take care of you or take you to the doctor if you needed it?
Yes No If yes, enter 1 ______

6. Were your parents ever separated or divorced?
Yes No If yes, enter 1 ______

7. Was your mother or stepmother (or father or stepfather):
Often or very often pushed, grabbed, slapped, or had something thrown at her (or him)?
or
Sometimes, often, or very often kicked, bitten, hit with a fist, or hit with something hard?
or
Ever hit repeatedly over at least a few minutes or threatened with a gun or knife?

Yes No If yes, enter 1 _______

8. Did you live with anyone who was a problem drinker or alcoholic, or who used street drugs?

Yes No If yes, enter 1 _______

9. Was a household member depressed or mentally ill, or did a household member attempt suicide?

Yes No If yes, enter 1 _______

10. Did a household member go to prison?

Yes No If yes, enter 1 _______

Now add up your Yes answers: _______ This is your ACE score.

Originally published in Felitti, V. J., Anda, R. F., Nordenberg, D., Williamson, D. F., Spitz, A. M., Edwards, V., Koss, M. P., & Marks, J. S. (1998). Relationship of Childhood Abuse and Household Dysfunction to Many of the Leading Causes of Death in Adults: The Adverse Childhood Experiences (ACE) Study. American Journal of Preventive Medicine, 14, 245–258.

ACE RESILIENCE QUESTIONNAIRE

Handout (page 41 in *Handouts & Homework*)

Many childhood experiences have been found to help cushion the impact of ACE scores. These usually help protect most people with four or more ACEs from developing negative outcomes.

1. I believe that my mother loved me when I was little.
   Definitely true Prob true Not sure Prob not true Def not true

2. I believe that my father loved me when I was little.
   Definitely true Prob true Not sure Prob not true Def not true

3. When I was little, other people helped my mother and father take care of me, and they seemed to love me.
   Definitely true Prob true Not sure Prob not true Def not true

4. I've heard that when I was an infant someone in my family enjoyed playing with me, and I enjoyed it too.
   Definitely true Prob true Not sure Prob not true Def not true

5. When I was a child, there were relatives in my family who made me feel better if I was sad or worried.
   Definitely true Prob true Not sure Prob not true Def not true

6. When I was a child, neighbors or my friends' parents seemed to like me.
   Definitely true Prob true Not sure Prob not true Def not true

7. When I was a child, teachers, coaches, youth leaders, or ministers were there to help me.
   Definitely true Prob true Not sure Prob not true Def not true

8. Someone in my family cared about how I was doing in school.
   Definitely true Prob true Not sure Prob not true Def not true

9. My family, neighbors, and friends talked often about making our lives better.
   Definitely true Prob true Not sure Prob not true Def not true

10. We had rules in our house and were expected to keep them.
    Definitely true Prob true Not sure Prob not true Def not true

11. When I felt really bad, I could almost always find someone I trusted to talk to.
    Definitely true Prob true Not sure Prob not true Def not true

12. As a youth, people noticed that I was capable and could get things done.

Definitely true   Prob true   Not sure   Prob not true   Def not true

13. I was independent and a go-getter.

Definitely true   Prob true   Not sure   Prob not true   Def not true

14. I believed that life is what you make it.

Definitely true   Prob true   Not sure   Prob not true   Def not true

How many of these 14 protective factors did I have as a child and youth? (How many of the 14 were circled "Definitely True" or "Prob True"?) ________

SESSION 4 HOMEWORK

Handout (page 43 in *Handouts & Homework*)

Fill out the What's My ACE Score? questionnaire again, this time from the perspective of one of your own children. If you do not have children, pick a child you know well and try to fill it out from his or her perspective.

Then do the same with the ACE Resilience Questionnaire, again from the child's perspective.

What's My ACE Score?

Prior to your 18th birthday:

1. Did a parent or other adult in the household often or very often . . .
Swear at you, insult you, put you down, or humiliate you?
or
Act in a way that made you afraid that you might be physically hurt?
Yes No If yes, enter 1 ________

2. Did a parent or other adult in the household often or very often . . .
Push, grab, slap, or throw something at you?
or
Ever hit you so hard that you had marks or were injured?
Yes No If yes, enter 1 ________

3. Did an adult or person at least 5 years older than you ever . . .
Touch or fondle you or have you touch their body in a sexual way?
or
Attempt or actually have oral, anal, or vaginal intercourse with you?
Yes No If yes, enter 1 ________

4. Did you often or very often feel that . . .
No one in your family loved you or thought you were important or special?
or
Your family didn't look out for each other, feel close to each other, or support each other?
Yes No If yes, enter 1 ________

5. Did you often or very often feel that . . .
You didn't have enough to eat, had to wear dirty clothes, and had no one to protect you?
or
Your parents were too drunk or high to take care of you or take you to the doctor if you needed it?
Yes No If yes, enter 1 ________

6. Was a biological parent ever lost to you through divorce, abandonment, or other reason?

Yes No If yes, enter 1 ______

7. Was your mother or stepmother (or father or stepfather):
Often or very often pushed, grabbed, slapped, or had something thrown at her (or him)?
or
Sometimes, often, or very often kicked, bitten, hit with a fist, or hit with something hard?
or
Ever hit repeatedly over at least a few minutes or threatened with a gun or knife?

Yes No If yes, enter 1 ______

8. Did you live with anyone who was a problem drinker or alcoholic, or who used street drugs?

Yes No If yes, enter 1 ______

9. Was a household member depressed or mentally ill, or did a household member attempt suicide?

Yes No If yes, enter 1 ______

10. Did a household member go to prison?

Yes No If yes, enter 1 ______

Now add up your Yes answers: ______ This is your ACE score.

ACE RESILIENCE QUESTIONNAIRE

Handout (page 45 in *Handouts & Homework*)

Many childhood experiences have been found to help cushion the impact of ACE scores. These usually help protect most people with four or more ACEs from developing negative outcomes.

1. I believe that my mother loved me when I was little.
   Definitely true Prob true Not sure Prob not true Def not true
2. I believe that my father loved me when I was little.
   Definitely true Prob true Not sure Prob not true Def not true
3. When I was little, other people helped my mother and father take care of me, and they seemed to love me.
   Definitely true Prob true Not sure Prob not true Def not true
4. I've heard that when I was an infant someone in my family enjoyed playing with me, and I enjoyed it, too.
   Definitely true Prob true Not sure Prob not true Def not true
5. When I was a child, there were relatives in my family who made me feel better if I was sad or worried.
   Definitely true Prob true Not sure Prob not true Def not true
6. When I was a child, neighbors or my friends' parents seemed to like me.
   Definitely true Prob true Not sure Prob not true Def not true
7. When I was a child, teachers, coaches, youth leaders, or ministers were there to help me.
   Definitely true Prob true Not sure Prob not true Def not true
8. Someone in my family cared about how I was doing in school.
   Definitely true Prob true Not sure Prob not true Def not true
9. My family, neighbors, and friends talked often about making our lives better.
   Definitely true Prob true Not sure Prob not true Def not true
10. We had rules in our house and were expected to keep them.
    Definitely true Prob true Not sure Prob not true Def not true
11. When I felt really bad, I could almost always find someone I trusted to talk to.
    Definitely true Prob true Not sure Prob not true Def not true

12. As a youth, people noticed that I was capable and could get things done.

Definitely true	Prob true	Not sure	Prob not true	Def not true

13. I was independent and a go-getter.

Definitely true	Prob true	Not sure	Prob not true	Def not true

14. I believed that life is what you make it.

Definitely true	Prob true	Not sure	Prob not true	Def not true

How many of these 14 protective factors did I have as a child and youth? (How many of the 14 were circled "Definitely True" or "Prob True"?) __________

Session 5

TRAUMA AND THINKING THE WORST

Materials:

Thinking the Worst
The Stories of Trauma

Program:

1. Ask each group member to report one gratitude (p. 59).
2. Focus on the mindfulness exercise (p. 60) for one minute.
3. Review the homework from the previous week.
4. Review the Weekly Check-Ins and use these to help guide the group discussion.
5. Review Thinking the Worst. The goal here is to help group members identify their own stories of blaming themselves for bad things that have happened to them and/or feeling doomed by the effects.
6. Now ask each of the group members to take a few minutes to complete the Stories of Trauma exercise. Since our group is not an intensive trauma treatment program, we just want to focus on the cognitive and narrative components of what they are telling themselves. Research has indicated that this is a very meaningful component of understanding and dealing with the effects of trauma.

TO FOCUS ON ALCOHOL AND DRUG ISSUES . . .

1. Discuss why people might turn to drugs or alcohol to deal with the effects of trauma.

THINKING THE WORST

Handout (page 47 in *Handouts & Homework*)

WHAT HAPPENED? WHAT ARE THE EFFECTS?	THE STORY YOU TELL YOURSELF
Trauma happened	■ *Nowhere is safe.* ■ *The next disaster will strike soon.*
Trauma happened *to me*	■ *I attract disaster.* ■ *People can see that I am a victim.* ■ *I deserve bad things to happen to me.* ■ *My personality has gotten worse.*
Irritability/anger/outbursts	■ *My marriage won't make it.* ■ *I can't trust myself with my own kids.*
Emotional numbing	■ *I'm dead inside.* ■ *I'll never relate okay to people again.*
Difficulty concentrating	■ *I'll never get over this.* ■ *My brain has been permanently damaged.* ■ *I'll lose my job.*
Positive reactions from others	■ *They think I'm too weak to cope—that's why they're trying to help me.* ■ *I don't want anyone's pity.*
Negative reactions from others	■ *They are judging me for what happened to me.* ■ *Nobody's there for me and never will be.* ■ *I can't rely on other people.*
Physical consequences	■ *My body is ruined.* ■ *I'll never lead a normal life again.*

THE STORIES OF TRAUMA

Handout (page 48 in *Handouts & Homework*)

If you can identify a traumatic event, take a few moments to make some notes about why you think this traumatic event occurred. For example: *I was sexually assaulted because of the way I dressed,* or *I did a lot of bad things as a kid, which is why I keep losing people who are close to me.*

It might be more comfortable to choose a more moderate event, like the breakup of a relationship (which practically everyone has experienced).

Also—remember that not all traumas are created equal. You may never have experienced extreme, dramatic trauma (like soldiers in combat zones or a violent childhood), but you have still been affected by the events in your own life.

You are not being asked to write specifics about the traumatic event. Write what you have been thinking you may have done that caused this event.

When you are done, we will discuss examples in the group. We want to make sure that no one in this group holds on to distorted reasons for why bad things have happened in their lives.

TRAUMATIC EVENT:

THIS HAPPENED BECAUSE . . .

SESSION 5 HOMEWORK

Handout (page 49 in *Handouts & Homework*)

Think of someone you know who has experienced a traumatic event, like a rape or growing up in a violent family. Write 100 words of what you would say to that person about why this happened. See if you can focus on the message that this was *not* his or her fault.

WHAT YOU WOULD SAY (100 WORDS):

Session 6

MAKING CHANGES AND SOCIAL SUPPORT

Materials:

Girlfriends and Social Support
House of Self-Worth and Empowerment
Video: *Men Don't Tell* (woman struggling with taking responsibility; 1:41:53–1:45:31 on DVD or 1:27:50–1:31:53 on YouTube)

Program:

1. Ask each group member to report one gratitude (p. 59).
2. Focus on the mindfulness exercise (p. 60) for one minute.
3. Review the homework from the previous week.
4. Review the Weekly Check-Ins and use these to help guide the group discussion.
5. Review each of the questions from Girlfriends and Social Support and discuss in group.
6. Reinforce the importance of positive self-esteem and talk about how self-esteem can be changed. Discuss the House of Self-Worth and Empowerment by drawing the house on the board, much like the House of Abuse from the New Member sessions. Ask the group members to generate information about areas of their lives that are important to them and that provide them with experiences of self-worth. As with the House of Abuse, the specific ideas should be clustered into different rooms of the house. Although these room names can be altered according to the particular group, suggested room names are the following:

   - Job
   - Social Life
   - Relaxation
   - Parenting
   - Spirituality
   - Partner Relationship

– Personal Skills (athletics, manual skills, intellectual abilities, etc.)
– Personal Integrity (examples of doing the right thing)

Then start asking the questions:

– *How does it feel to live in this House?*
– *How do the rooms strengthen each other?*
– *What do you need to do to make sure that these rooms are filled?*

And, the final question:

– *What do these rooms support? What is on the roof?*

The answer is "self-worth and empowerment."

7. Watch the video clip from *Men Don't Tell* as an introduction to the Making Changes discussion. *What did it take for this woman to realize she had changes to make? How is she still resisting this?*

TO FOCUS ON ALCOHOL AND DRUG ISSUES . . .

1. Discuss times when friends or family have ever told them they have a problem with alcohol and/or drugs.
2. Discuss ways in which they have tried to make changes in their alcohol and/or drug use.

GIRLFRIENDS AND SOCIAL SUPPORT

Handout (page 50 in *Handouts & Homework*)

Adapted with permission from Koonin, M., Cabarcas, A., & Geffner, R. (2002). Women Ending Abusive/Violent Episodes Respectfully (WEAVER) Manual. San Diego CA: Family Violence and Sexual Assault Institute.

Women who have been most supportive in your life are:

What actions did these women do that made you feel supported?

What qualities have you admired in other women?

When do you or your friends justify violence? (For example: when your partner is caught cheating, when a friend is intimate with your partner, when someone threatens your child)

Have you disclosed to your friends that you are in a domestic violence group or have been aggressive to your partner?

Have your friends encouraged your violence or helped you validate it?

Women tend to be very supportive of one another. Do you have friends that will honestly challenge you when you are in the wrong or acting out of hand?

THE HOUSE OF SELF-WORTH AND EMPOWERMENT

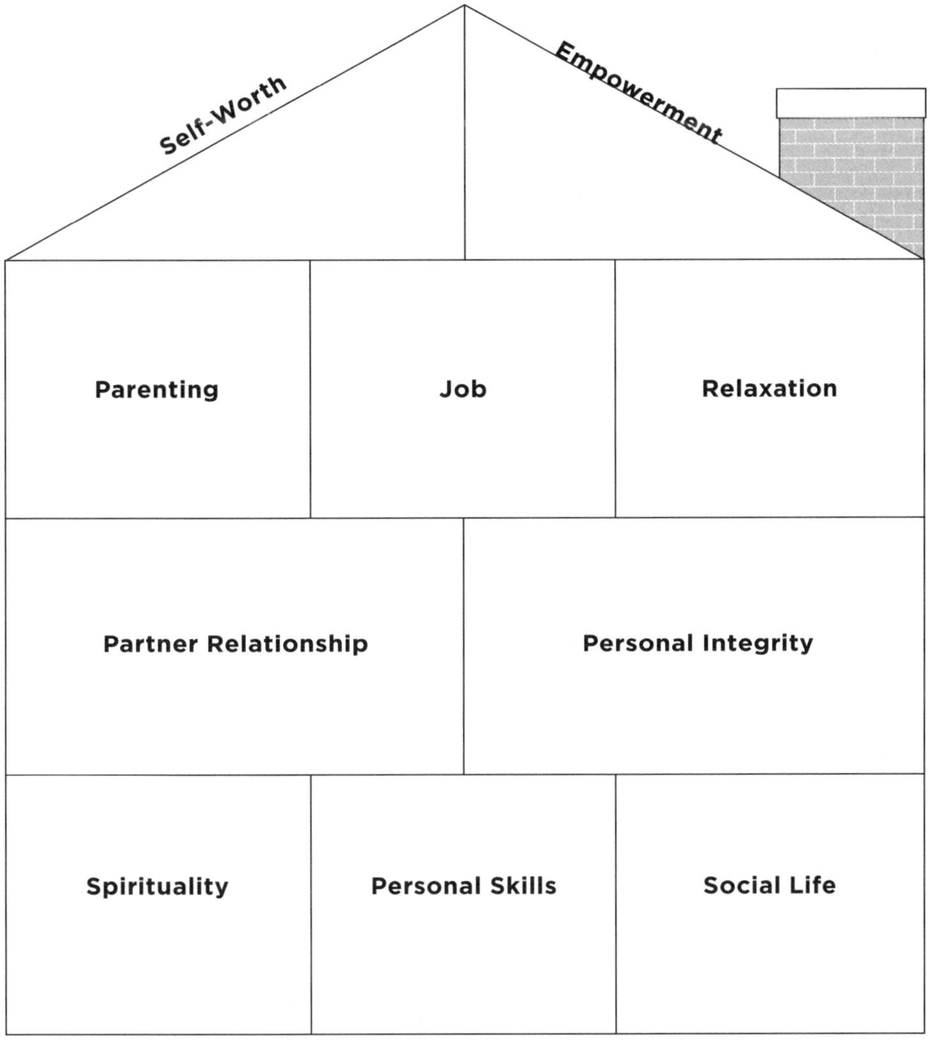

SESSION 6 HOMEWORK

Handout (page 52 in *Handouts & Homework*)

MAKING CHANGES

Adapted with permission from Koonin, M., Cabarcas, A., & Geffner, R. (2002). Women Ending Abusive/Violent Episodes Respectfully (WEAVER) Manual. San Diego CA: Family Violence and Sexual Assault Institute.

Check any boxes to the right that are goals of yours (and fill in the specifics in that box if you see a . . .). Then make notes about when you expect to see progress on this, what seems to be in the way, and what resources you need to move forward.

GOAL	BY WHEN?	OBSTACLES?	RESOURCES NEEDED?
Finish school			
Do work as . . .			
Be recognized as . . .			
Be in a stable relationship			
Have children			

People I want to know . . .			
Places I want to see . . .			
Skills I want to learn . . .			
Add or lose ___ pounds			
Other goals . . .			

PART VII

REVISING PERSONAL STORIES

Session 7

SELF-TALK AND PERSONAL STORIES

Materials:

Bad Rap
Bad Rap Quiz
Stories We Tell Ourselves

Program:

1. Ask each group member to report one gratitude (p. 59).
2. Focus on the mindfulness exercise (p. 60) for one minute.
3. Review the homework from the previous week.
4. Review the Weekly Check-Ins and use these to help guide the group discussion.
5. Introduce a basic working model of self-talk. Use the ABCDE model, emphasizing how the way we interpret events can determine the way we feel and act (from Wexler, 1991).

   A. **Objective Event:** This is the initial event. Your partner comes home and says, *I hate my job!*
   B. **Self-Talk:** You might say to yourself, *He's trying to tell me that he doesn't want to work so hard and that I should be making more money so he shouldn't have to!*
   C. **Feelings and Behavior:** If you interpreted it this way, you would probably be critical of him, or act defensive, or sulk, or worry. Maybe you would say to him, *Quit complaining! You think you're the only one who has it tough?*
   D. **New Self-Talk:** Maybe there is another way to interpret what he said. Maybe he was just tired and needed some support, like we all do. Maybe it was not intended as a message or critical comment. You might be saying to yourself, *It sounds like he's had a rotten day. What can I do to help?*
   E. **New Feelings and Behavior:** If you interpreted it this way, you might say, *Let's talk about it.* Or you might try to cheer him up. Or you might just whisk the kids off into another room and let him be alone for a while. Your response

would be based on what you thought he might need, rather than defending yourself against a perceived attack.

6. Now explain the seven categories of Bad Rap. Teach the names of the categories and go through the different examples. Ask the group members to come up with examples of their own.

7. Quiz group members with the Bad Rap Quiz, to make sure that they get the idea. Try turning this into a *Family Feud* contest, with different teams competing for the right answer. If one team identifies the correct category for the statement, award a point. This team then has the opportunity to rephrase the statement so that it reflects productive or realistic self-talk, worth an additional point. If a team answers incorrectly, the other team can try, until one of the teams gets it right. Make sure that they learn how to revise the faulty self-talk into sentences that would be more realistic self-talk.

   This is designed to be entertaining and engaging, with one primary purpose. This purpose should be repeated and emphasized throughout this session and others: ***We want you to see how powerful your self-talk is in determining your emotions and your behaviors in any situation. And we want you to see that it is possible, in a lot of these situations, to change the self-talk and end up with emotions and behaviors that do not mess you up so much. This is another example of making YOU powerful—not over others, but over yourself.***

8. Review More Stories We Tell Ourselves and discuss.

TO FOCUS ON ALCOHOL AND DRUG ISSUES . . .

1. Discuss how "bad rap" cognitions can make someone more likely to use.

- *I've had a bad day—I deserve to have a drink!*
- *It's his fault that I'm getting high today!*

BAD RAP

Handout (page 54 in *Handouts & Homework*)

Adapted with permission from Wexler, D. B. (1991). The adolescent self: Strategies for self-management, self-soothing, and self-esteem in adolescence. New York: Norton.

1. **BLACK AND WHITE:** Seeing things as all or nothing: *never/always/everyone.*

   A good woman is always there to help.
   You're either on my side or you're not.
   You can't trust men.

2. **MINIMIZING:** Downplaying your achievements.

   Even though I finally made supervisor, it's no big deal.
   I did well, but so did a lot of other people.
   My counselor just gives me good feedback because she's paid to say it.

3. **MIND READING:** Assuming that others think something without checking it out.

   I know my boss hates me—he gave me a dirty look.
   He's avoiding me—he must be pretty mad.
   My partner didn't call me today—she must not care about me.

4. **AWFULIZING:** Predicting that things will turn out awful for you.

   My boss will never trust me again.
   I know I'm not going to make it through this place.
   Wow, she is so good at that—I'll never be able to do it that well!

5. **ERROR IN BLAMING:** Unfairly blaming yourself—or others.

   It's all my fault, or *It's all your fault.*
   It's my fault my son is shy.
   You always mess everything up for me.

6. **DOWN-PUTTING:** Making too much of your mistakes (opposite of **MINIMIZING**).

   I failed this test; I must be dumb.
   I'm in counseling; there must be something really wrong with me.
   She doesn't like me, so there must be something really wrong with me.

7. **EMOTIONAL REASONING:** Concluding that if you *feel* a certain way about yourself, then it must be true.

   Since I feel bad about myself, I must be a bad person.
   I feel rejected, so everybody must be rejecting me.
   Since I feel guilty, I must have done something wrong.

BAD RAP QUIZ

Handout (page 55 in *Handouts & Homework*)

Adapted with permission from Wexler, D. B. (1991). The adolescent self: Strategies for self-management, self-soothing, and self-esteem in adolescence. New York: Norton.

(Please note that the answers to the quiz items are in parentheses—these numbers are NOT included in the handouts for group members.)

1. The counselor told me I'm doing better, but I know he tells that to everybody. (2)
2. Ever since that really handsome guy Paul hurt me, I know that good-looking men can't be trusted. (1)
3. If I'm angry, there must be something to be angry about. (7)
4. Nothing's ever going to work out for me. (4)
5. It's your fault we never do anything fun. (5)
6. My parents got divorced; it must have been something about me. (5)
7. I sometimes don't get things right, so I must be lazy or stupid. (6)
8. I feel lonely, so I guess nobody likes me. (7)
9. That supervisor shows me no respect; nobody in this organization cares a damn about me.

STORIES WE TELL OURSELVES

Handout **(page 56 in *Handouts & Homework*)**

THE OLD STORY	THE NEW STORY
If he forgets my birthday, it means he doesn't love me.	*I feel hurt when he forgets my birthday, but there are other ways he shows me he loves me.*
I can't believe my son violated curfew. He's always pushing the limits with me—and I have to teach him a lesson!	*I'm glad he's safe—in the morning I can talk calmly with him and figure out what happened and what to do.*
He always has to win every argument. He just wants to show how he's smarter than I am!	*He does have strong opinions, but so do I. I don't always have to change my mind—or his.*
She's trying to start a fight with me to make me act crazy! She wants to get me arrested!	*I don't have to get into a fight with her, and I don't have to choose violence.*
My daughter always expects me to help her with her homework—she's such a baby!	*Learning to read is hard. I'm glad she turns to me for help, and I'm glad I can help her.*
If he doesn't listen to me, I'll throw the remote at him—it's the only way to get his attention!	*Relationships are not always easy, and violence isn't going to bring us closer. I don't want to make a bad situation even worse.*

SESSION 7 HOMEWORK

Handout **(page 57 in *Handouts & Homework*)**

Go back to the Stories We Tell Ourselves chart. Fill out three more examples (from your personal experience) that could go on this list.

1.

2.

3.

Session 8

JEALOUSY AND MISINTERPRETATIONS

Materials:

Jealousy: Taming the Green-Eyed Monster
Video: *When Your Partner Doesn't Trust You* (https://www.youtube.com/watch?v=K9hznPEcRSg)
Stories of Jealousy: I Knew I Was Right

Program:

1. Ask each group member to report one gratitude (p. 59).
2. Focus on the mindfulness exercise (p. 60) for one minute.
3. Review the homework from the previous week.
4. Review the Weekly Check-Ins and use these to help guide the group discussion.
5. One of the strongest, most consistent traits of people who act abusively in relationships is jealousy. Sometimes the jealousy is based on reality, and sometimes it is entirely fantasy—stemming from the insecurity of the person or distortions based on use of alcohol or other drugs.
6. Read through the stories from Jealousy: Taming the Green-Eyed Monster and discuss, with questions such as these:
   - *Have you had thoughts or feelings similar to any of the people in the stories?*
   - *What have you found that works to reduce jealousy?*
   - *What constructive self-talk can you use to combat jealousy?*
   - *How would you respectfully ask your partner for behavior change to reduce jealousy?*
7. Play the *When Your Partner Doesn't Trust You* video and discuss, using questions such as these:
   - *Have there ever been jealousy issues in your relationship over a text or something else on social media?*
   - *How else could the woman have handled her anxieties?*

- *Is there anything the guy could have done differently or better to handle his girlfriend's suspicions?*
- *What do you think about the counselor saying, "Don't let insecurity ruin something amazing"?*

8. Review Stories of Jealousy: I Knew I Was Right and discuss the cognitive distortions and bad rap.

TO FOCUS ON ALCOHOL AND DRUG ISSUES . . .

1. Discuss how jealousy can often be triggered by cognitive distortions that are exaggerated by alcohol or drugs.
2. Discuss ways in which judgment and decision making are impaired when someone is intoxicated, so that they might overreact (sometimes violently) when they feel threatened.

JEALOUSY: TAMING THE GREEN-EYED MONSTER

Handout (page 58 in *Handouts & Homework*)

Jealousy is one of those emotions that can tie our stomach in knots in a hurry. A little bit of jealousy is natural, especially when we fear losing someone close to us. Jealousy becomes a problem when . . .

- we spend too much energy worrying about losing a loved one
- we let jealousy build, and we try to control someone else through aggression
- we stifle a relationship by placing extreme restrictions on our partner

Tania got herself really worked up whenever she went to a party with her husband, Peter. Tania was afraid that he would find another woman more attractive and exciting than she was. She usually picked some sort of fight with him after the party, without ever telling him what she was really upset about.

One day after one of these fights, Tania was thinking about how upset she made herself with jealousy. She tried to look at the situation in a more objective way—the way an outside observer would. After a while she was able to say to herself, *My husband is very attractive, and it is only natural that women will sometimes find him attractive too. That doesn't mean I'm going to lose him. He hasn't given me any reason to doubt him. My fears and anger come from doubting my self-worth. If other women like him, it only confirms what I already know—and that's positive.*

Alicia's jealousy was even stronger than Tania's. She would question her boyfriend at length when he came home, asking where he had been, who he had been with, and the details of his activities. She checked out his text messages and his phone bills. She would get urges to follow him everywhere or demand that he stay home. It seemed that the more she questioned him, the more she disbelieved him.

It was after hearing her friend talk about wanting to have an affair that Alicia realized what was happening. The times when she was most suspicious of her boyfriend were the times when *she* was actually thinking about other men.

Now when she noticed jealousy, she asked herself, *Am I just thinking that he's cheating on me because I'm feeling guilty?*

Amy found that the best way for her to tame the monster was to let her girlfriend know when she felt jealous. She felt very relieved being able to talk about it. Sometimes they could laugh about it together. Instead of responding with ridicule, she seemed to respect her more. Both of them went on to say what behavior from each other they could and could not tolerate—affairs, flirting, having friends, and so on. They were able to work out some contracts that specified the limits of the relationship.

What **Tania, Alicia,** and **Amy** learned about taming jealousy was the following:

1. Some jealousy is normal, and it's best to talk about it rather than hide it.
2. People can choose to see their partner's attractiveness and behavior in the most negative possible way—or they can turn it around and see it in a way that is not such a threat.

3. It will help people to ask, *Is my jealousy coming from my guilt about my own fantasies or behavior?*

4. Women have the right to request and contract for some specific limits on their partner's behavior (not thoughts), and men have the same right.*

* Thanks to Daniel G. Saunders, PhD, for contributing many of these ideas.

STORIES OF JEALOUSY: I KNEW I WAS RIGHT

Handout (page 60 in *Handouts & Homework*)

Maria had been cheated on in the past. She was "sure" that men couldn't be trusted. It seemed like all her friends had been through the same thing.

She knew it was just a matter of time until her boyfriend Antonio would betray her, and she knew that she needed to watch him carefully. When she did his laundry, she'd check his pockets for receipts and phone numbers. When she drove his car, she'd check the mileage to see how far he had gone. She figured out the password for his phone and email and checked it regularly without him knowing about it.

If he put on nice clothes and cologne, she would grill him about where he was going, because she knew that he must be getting dressed up to meet another woman.

Eventually, Antonio got really tired of Maria checking on him all the time—and he actually began seeing someone else who wasn't so jealous and insecure. Maria's story about men was confirmed: this proved that men couldn't be trusted, and that she was right—again—about this one. She began following him around to see who this other woman was and whether she was prettier than Maria.

Sometimes we actually want something to go wrong in our relationships—just so we can say that we knew we were right all along.

SESSION 8 HOMEWORK

Handout (page 61 in *Handouts & Homework*)

Record three experiences of jealousy over the next week. These can include anything from high levels (like seeing your husband or partner flirting with someone else) to low (like observing your supervisor give approval to someone else). If you do not notice any this week, recall experiences from previous weeks.

1.

2.

3.

Session 9

SWITCH!

Materials:

Switch!

Program:

1. Ask each group member to report one gratitude (p. 59).
2. Focus on the mindfulness exercise (p. 60) for one minute.
3. Review the homework from the previous week.
4. Review the Weekly Check-Ins and use these to help guide the group discussion.
5. Ask one group member (the most veteran in the group) to choose a disturbing situation from the past—*perhaps the incident that got you here*—or any other time when she reacted with verbal or physical aggression. Remember that you are trying to assess the members' ability to examine personal responsibility—and new options—for abusive behavior.

Lead the group member through the steps of Switch! This is a very important opportunity to assess how well she is able to examine herself and integrate new ideas.

The first two steps of Switch! are used to **identify the problem situation** and **identify the self-talk**. Make a chart with two columns on the board, one labeled OLD SELF-TALK and the other labeled NEW SELF-TALK.

- **OLD SELF-TALK:** The first step is for the target member to describe the destructive self-talk she was having building up to the problem situation. For example:

  – *He completely forgot about my work party.*
  – *He never pays any attention to me.*
  – *He's always thinking about himself.*
  – *He's never there when I need him.*
  – *I* know *he's got someone else on the side.*

As she comes up with these, write them in the left-hand column (OLD SELF-TALK). Ask the group members for suggestions about the self-talk that might belong there. If she agrees, put them on the board. If she says it doesn't sound right, then it doesn't go on the list. You should end up with at least four or five core statements.

- **NEW SELF-TALK:** The next step focuses on developing new self-talk. For example:

  - *I know he's got a lot going on.*
  - *I hate it when he doesn't remember stuff that's important to me, but I can talk to him about it, and he usually takes me seriously and feels bad.*
  - *There are probably plenty of times when he feels like I'm not paying attention to what's important to him, too.*
  - *This definitely bothers me—but there's so many other ways he comes through for me.*

As she comes up with these, this time write them in the right-hand column (NEW SELF-TALK). Ask the group members for suggestions about the self-talk that might belong there. If she agrees, put them on the board. If she says it doesn't sound right, then it doesn't go on the list. You should end up with at least four or five core statements.

Now the reframing begins. The target member is asked to **imagine that she is back in the problem situation**. Ask her to begin stating aloud the old self-talk which led to the destructive outcome. When the group leader gives the command, the group—in very loud unison—yells **"SWITCH!"** Then she starts saying the new self-talk and picturing how this would have led to different emotions and very different behavior. (Group members usually love to yell this, so definitely encourage it!)

6. Here are some key follow-up questions:

   - *If somehow you had been able to use the new self-talk back then, do you think you would have been busted on a domestic violence charge? Do you think this would have led to a different outcome?*
   - *Do you really think you could use this new self-talk in the future? What might get in your way? (If she says she is confident she can do it, great. If she says she is not sure, tell her you really appreciate her honesty, and that we know making these changes is not easy to do).*

7. Each round of Switch! should take about 10 minutes. Try to get to as many group members as you can. **Note: This is meant to be entertaining—and to provide a shock to the individual's typical self-talk patterns!**

TO FOCUS ON ALCOHOL AND DRUG ISSUES . . .

1. Compare the old self-talk that takes place while under the influence of alcohol or drugs to the new self-talk that is likely to be more clear thinking.
2. Identify ways in which group members have been more effective in managing their destructive behaviors when they are clean and sober.
3. Content of the Switch! session may focus on the decision to use in addition to the decision to be aggressive or violent.

SWITCH!

Handout (page 62 in *Handouts & Homework*)

1. ***What went wrong?***
   a. Who was involved? When was it? Where was it? Describe exactly what was happening. Be specific and objective.
   b. Replay this like a movie. What exactly did you do and say?
   c. Other group members should help by asking questions so the movie is very clear.

2. ***What was my OLD SELF-TALK?***
   a. What was your self-talk before, during, and after the situation?
   b. Freeze the frame of this movie so you can stop at different points and identify the self-talk.
   c. With the group's help, analyze the self-defeating or unproductive self-talk.

3. ***What NEW SELF-TALK could I have used?***
   a. What would you like to have said to yourself instead in this situation?
   b. Brainstorm with the group for alternative self-talk.

4. ***The Switch!***
   a. Put yourself back in the problem situation.
   b. Practice the OLD SELF-TALK out loud (see the notes on the board).
   c. When the group yells out "Switch!" try using your NEW SELF-TALK instead (see the notes on the board).

5. ***What do you think? What does the group think?***
   a. Do you think this would have led to a different outcome?
   b. Do you really think you could use this new self-talk in the future? What might get in your way?

SESSION 9 HOMEWORK

Handout (page 63 in *Handouts & Homework*)

Do your own Switch! exercise. Pick out another time when you wish you had not reacted the way you did in your relationship.

SITUATION AND YOUR REACTION

OLD SELF-TALK

NEW SELF-TALK

PREDICTED NEW REACTION

PART VIII

RELATIONSHIP SKILLS

Session 10

EMPOWERMENT, ASSERTIVENESS, AND BOUNDARIES

Materials:

Assertiveness
What Is Assertive Behavior?
Boundary Violations

Program:

1. Ask each group member to report one gratitude (p. 59).
2. Focus on the mindfulness exercise (p. 60) for one minute.
3. Review the homework from the previous week.
4. Review the Weekly Check-Ins and use these to help guide the group discussion.
5. Review Assertiveness and What Is Assertive Behavior? as a way of giving basic education about assertiveness and of getting the women to become aware of their own degree of assertiveness.

   Write the Assertiveness definition on the board: **ASSERTIVENESS: TAKING CARE OF YOUR OWN NEEDS, THOUGHTS, AND FEELINGS—IN A WAY THAT IS LEAST LIKELY TO MAKE THE OTHER PERSON FEEL ATTACKED OR ACT DEFENSIVE**.

   Refer back to this definition again and again as you review examples. In future sessions, give the group members a pop quiz on this definition.

   While discussing the five types of behaviors in the first handout, encourage the women to give examples. The group leaders should give other examples, then model and role-play the different assertive behaviors. Encourage the women to think of benefits of assertiveness for them personally or for the relationship.

   Remind the group members that these are tools, not rules. Sometimes it makes sense to be passive, and sometimes (as in self-defense situations) it even makes sense to be aggressive. These tools are all designed primarily for relationships that we *care* about—relationships that we want to preserve as respectfully as possible.

6. Review Boundary Violations and discuss.
7. Explain the Line in the Sand homework and assign.

TO FOCUS ON ALCOHOL AND DRUG ISSUES . . .

1. Discuss how use of substances and addiction affects communication styles, leading to extremes of passivity/withdrawal or aggression.

ASSERTIVENESS

Handout (page 64 in *Handouts & Homework*)

ASSERTIVENESS: TAKING CARE OF YOUR OWN NEEDS, THOUGHTS, AND FEELINGS—IN A WAY THAT IS LEAST LIKELY TO MAKE THE OTHER PERSON FEEL ATTACKED OR ACT DEFENSIVE

1. **Assertive.** This behavior involves knowing what you feel and want. It also involves expressing your feelings and needs directly and honestly without violating the rights of others. At all times you are accepting responsibility for your feelings and actions.
    - *"It bothered me when you were late coming back from shopping, because I had to rush off to work."*
2. **Aggressive.** You attack your partner, act controlling, provoke a confrontation, and maybe even get violent. The consequences could be destructive to others as well as yourself.
    - *"What the hell's wrong with you? All you ever think about is yourself!"*
3. **Passive.** You withdraw, become anxious, and avoid confrontation. You let others think for you, make decisions for you, and tell you what to do. You feel resentful but don't express it or deal with it. You feel like it's useless: either you don't deserve any better, or nobody will ever listen to you anyway. Usually you will become depressed, and you may believe that your partner is purposely trying to take advantage of you—but you do nothing about the situation.
    - *"That's OK, whatever you want."*
4. **Passive-Aggressive.** In this behavior you are not direct in relating to people, do not accept what is happening—but will retaliate in an indirect manner. This type of behavior can cause confusion. The other person feels stung but can't be exactly sure how or why. And you can act like you have done nothing at all—and imply that your partner is just too sensitive.
    - You act cold to your partner, then pretend like nothing's wrong when he or she asks you about it.
    - A woman feels unappreciated by her husband and "forgets" to give him a message.
    - A woman makes some "joking" comment about her partner's weight.
5. SPECIAL CATEGORY: **Passive-Assertive.** There are plenty of situations when someone assertively chooses to be passive. And this is often a good choice. When one person is in a bad mood and complaining about things that are not really fair, sometimes—in the most successful of relationships—the other partner just chooses to let it go. The same is true when an employee chooses to keep her mouth shut even when she doesn't like an office policy (thanks to Genevieve Olucha, PhD, for this concept).

WHAT IS ASSERTIVE BEHAVIOR?

Handout (page 65 in *Handouts & Homework*)

1. Asking for what you want but not being demanding.
2. Expressing feelings.
3. Genuinely expressing feedback or compliments to others and accepting them.
4. Disagreeing without being aggressive.
5. Asking questions and getting information from others.
6. Using I-messages and "I feel" statements without being judgmental or blaming.
7. Making eye contact during a conversation (unless this is inappropriate in the person's culture).

EXAMPLES:

1. *Can you give me some feedback about how I handled the kids' homework tonight?*
2. *I feel embarrassed when you tease me about my weight in front of my friends.*
3. *Mom, I know you want us to call more often, but I don't think you realize how busy we both are.*
4. *Corey, I just saw your report card, and I'm concerned. Let's sit down and talk about this together.*
5. *Maria, I'd like to talk about this later after we've both cooled off.*
6. Look your partner in the eye and say, *I really care about you. Let's work this out.*

BOUNDARY VIOLATIONS

Handout (page 66 in *Handouts & Homework*)

Adapted with permission from Turner (Fischer, K. L. & McGrane, M. F. [1997]. Journey beyond abuse: A step-by-step guide to facilitating women's domestic abuse groups. St Paul: Amherst H. Wilder Foundation.).

TIME:

- Expecting partner to cease current activity in order to immediately meet the other partner's demands
- Setting a curfew for a partner
- Starting a fight as partner is leaving for work or another appointment

SPACE:

- Not treating purses, wallets, files, drawers, and so on as private space
- Making accusations about what your partner has been doing while away
- Getting too close physically when in conflict

PROPERTY:

- Taking or using things without asking
- Destruction of personal property, meant to be personally hurtful
- Taking car keys to prevent partner from leaving

PRIVACY:

- Reading/checking partner's mail, voicemail, or journal
- Listening in on phone conversations
- Demanding that partner account for all her/his time

SEXUAL:

- Lack of privacy in bathroom
- Making negative comments regarding partner's size and shape
- Not accepting when a partner says no to sex

FEELINGS:

- Telling partner what he/she should feel
- Calling partner wrong, ridiculous, bad, overly sensitive, and so on, because of how they feel
- Taunting, mimicking, or belittling partner for feelings

Recognizing boundary violations against yourself (and your own boundary violations of others) is the first step toward establishing more healthful boundaries.

SESSION 10 HOMEWORK

Handout (page 67 in *Handouts & Homework*)

WHERE IS YOUR LINE IN THE SAND?

We all put up with lots of imperfections and annoying behaviors in our partners. The capacity to do this is usually a sign of personal strength, maturity, and love. But some unacceptable behaviors are so profoundly unacceptable that they should never be tolerated, or at least never tolerated more than once. When you draw a line in the sand, you are making a contract with yourself that you will absolutely leave this relationship under certain conditions. When you put it in writing, and you sign it, you are more likely to have the perspective and courage to follow through if the situation actually happens.

I will have no choice but to leave my partner if he or she ever (cheats on me, hits me, abuses the children, lies to me about gambling, makes another suicide attempt, visits child porn sites, etc.):

1. ______________________________
2. ______________________________
3. ______________________________

I will have no choice but to leave my partner if he or she ever no longer (talks to me for weeks on end, tries to find a job, allows me to talk on the phone with my friends or family, etc.):

1. ______________________________
2. ______________________________
3. ______________________________

______________________________ ______________
Your signature Date

Session 11

ASKING FOR CHANGE

Materials:

Respectful Feedback
Asking for Change
How We Talk Ourselves Out of It

Program:

1. Ask each group member to report one gratitude (p. 59).
2. Focus on the mindfulness exercise (p. 60) for one minute.
3. Review the homework from the previous week.
4. Review the Weekly Check-Ins and use these to help guide the group discussion.
5. Review Respectful Feedback and discuss.
6. Review the Asking for Change handout. Role-play and discuss the examples. **Remind the group members that the theme here is respectful communication—which is more likely to bring about the relationship they truly want.**
7. Review How We Talk Ourselves Out of It and discuss.

TO FOCUS ON ALCOHOL AND DRUG ISSUES . . .

1. Discuss the effects of substance abuse on communication patterns involving secrets, dishonesty, and blaming.
2. Discuss how trying to ask for behavioral change from other people is less likely to succeed if they mistrust the person because of a history of alcohol or drug use.

RESPECTFUL FEEDBACK

Handout **(page 68 in *Handouts & Homework*)**

Adapted with permission from Koonin, M., Cabarcas, A., & Geffner, R. (2002). Women Ending Abusive/Violent Episodes Respectfully (WEAVER) Manual. San Diego CA: Family Violence and Sexual Assault Institute.

The purpose of respectful feedback is to offer your partner some valuable information—not to make them feel attacked or beat up.

1. Feedback focuses on describing rather than judging behavior.
2. Feedback is specific rather than general.
3. Feedback takes into account the needs of both the receiver and giver of the feedback.
4. Feedback is directed toward behavior that the receiver can do something about.
5. Feedback is well timed.
6. Feedback is checked to ensure clear communication.
7. Both the giver and the receiver need to check with others, if possible, the accuracy of the feedback. Is this one person's impression or an impression shared by others?
8. Feedback contains only the amount of information that the receiver can tolerate.

ASKING FOR CHANGE

Handout (page 69 in *Handouts & Homework*)

One method to use when you want to communicate your feelings, meanings, and intentions is I-messages. I-messages are specific, nonjudgmental, and focus on you. In contrast, you-messages are hostile, blaming, and focused on the other person. Reframing you-messages into I-messages can help you communicate—because the other person will not feel attacked.

Construct I-messages by using these phrases:

1. **When you** (just describe, don't blame).
2. **I feel** (state the feeling) **because** (explain in more detail).
   Note: Using the word *because* with an explanation can help by giving the other person more information to understand you.
3. **I wish** (specify a new behavior that you would like the other person to use instead).
4. **And if you can do that, I will** (explain how the other person will benefit).

The different parts of the I-message do not have to be delivered in exact order. The important thing is to keep the focus on yourself and to stay away from blame.

- *When you take long phone calls during dinner,*
- *I get angry because I begin to think you don't want to talk to me.*
- *I wish you would tell whoever's calling that you'll call back because we're in the middle of dinner.*
- *And if you can do that, I'll make sure not to hassle you about being on the phone later.*

- *When you don't come home or call,*
- *I get worried that something has happened to you.*
- *I would really like you to call me if you're going to be late.*
- *And if you can do that, I promise not to have an attitude when you get home.*

- *When you yell at me right in the middle of a busy time at work,*
- *I get so rattled that I end up making more mistakes.*
- *I wish that you would lighten up when you know that I'm busy.*
- *And if you can do that, I will be a lot easier to work with.*

CLASSIC MISTAKES:

1. Being too vague: *When you are selfish . . .*
2. Putting down character (*You are so controlling!*) instead of a specific behavior (*Last night it bothered me that you gave me so many instructions about the kids*).
3. Saying, *I feel that you . . .* instead of *I feel* (emotion).
4. Not offering a specific and realistic new behavior (*I want you to become a more outgoing person*).

HOW WE TALK OURSELVES OUT OF IT

Handout (page 70 in *Handouts & Homework*)

1. *I can't stand it if my partner gets upset with me.*
   NEW STORY:

2. *If I ask for help, I must be too needy.*
   NEW STORY:

3. *I don't deserve to get what I want or need.*
   NEW STORY:

4. *If I have to ask, it means he (or she) doesn't love me.*
   NEW STORY:

5. *I must really be a loser if I can't fix this myself.*
   NEW STORY:

6. *Making this request is a really pushy (bad, self-centered, selfish) thing to do.*
   NEW STORY:

7. *It doesn't make any difference. I don't care anyway.*
   NEW STORY:

8. *Obviously the problem is just in my head. If I would just think differently, I wouldn't have to bother someone else.*
   NEW STORY:

9. *Saying no is always a selfish thing.*
   NEW STORY:

SESSION 11 HOMEWORK

Handout (page 71 in *Handouts & Homework*)

How often do you take full responsibility for what you do and say?

Record two situations when you heard yourself say any of these types of statements (out loud or just in your own head):

- *You made me . . .*
- *It's your fault that I . . .*
- *If you (or he or she) weren't so XXXX, I wouldn't have to . . .*
- *I only did XXXX because I was drunk.*
- *He made me so mad that I had to . . .*

SITUATION #1:

What You Told Yourself That Gave Up Your Responsibility:

What You Could Have Said To Yourself Instead:

SITUATION #2:

What You Told Yourself That Gave Up Your Responsibility:

What You Could Have Said To Yourself Instead:

Session 12

EMPATHY AND ACTIVE LISTENING

Materials:

Active Listening
Communication Roadblocks
Video: *The Power of Empathy* (https://www.youtube.com/watch?v=jz1g1SpD9Zo)

Program:

1. Ask each group member to report one gratitude (p. 59).
2. Focus on the mindfulness exercise" (p. 60) for one minute.
3. Review the homework from the previous week.
4. Review the Weekly Check-Ins and use these to help guide the group discussion.
5. Review the Active Listening handout. Explain the basic concepts, then model and role-play active listening based on the different examples.
6. Play video: *The Power of Empathy*. Discuss the value of simple reflective listening.
7. Review the Communication Roadblocks handout and discuss.

TO FOCUS ON ALCOHOL AND DRUG ISSUES . . .

1. Discuss how intoxication and patterns of abuse can interfere with the ability to hear what another person is saying and to offer active listening responses.

ACTIVE LISTENING

Handout **(page 72 in *Handouts & Homework*)**

Active listening is a communication technique that encourages the other person to continue speaking. It also enables you to be certain you understand what the other person is saying. It's a way of checking it out. It's called active listening because you not only listen but also actively let the other person know that you have really heard him or her.

A. Active listening involves PARAPHRASING.

Paraphrasing is stating in your own words what you think the other person has said.

- *You* sound *really* (feeling) *about* (situation).
- *You must really feel . . .* (state a feeling).
- *What I hear you saying is* ____________.

B. Active listening also involves CLARIFYING.

Clarifying involves asking questions to get more information.

Clarifying helps you hear more specifics about the situation and feelings.

Clarifying also lets the other person know you are interested in what he or she is saying.

- *So tell me what happened that got you so upset.*
- *How did you feel when that happened?*

C. Active listening often involves PERSONALIZING.

Personalizing involves offering a personal example of feeling the same thing or being in the same situation.

- *I think I know what you mean. I've been there too.*
- *I felt the same way when I lost my job. I think everyone does.*

Personalizing helps the other person feel less alone, and it implies that someone else has experienced this and has recovered from it.

Personalizing can be harmful if you talk too much about yourself and steal the spotlight from the person who needs it.

- *You think that was bad? Listen to what happened to me!*

D. Active listening does not mean cheering up, defending yourself, judging the person, or just repeating back exactly what was said.

- *All I ever do is the dirty work around here!*
- *Oh, come on, it's a hot day, you're just in a bad mood, don't worry about it.*

You can't trust anyone around this place!

- *Now, now, it's okay. It's all going to be better—I'll take care of it for you.*

I'm really worried that my family is going to be mad at me for dropping out of school.

- *You shouldn't feel that way.*

I keep trying to talk to you about how to handle the kids and you never listen to me!

- *I'm in charge! No more discussion!*

This place is really disgusting.

- *It sounds like you think this place is really disgusting.*

Some keys to being a GOOD ACTIVE LISTENER:

- Good eye contact, leaning slightly forward, reinforcing by nodding or paraphrasing, clarifying by asking questions
- Avoiding distractions
- Trying to really understand what the other person is really saying

COMMUNICATION ROADBLOCKS

Handout (page 74 in *Handouts & Homework*)

Adapted with permission from Koonin, M., Cabarcas, A., & Geffner, R. (2002). Women ending abusive/violent episodes respectfully (WEAVER) manual. San Diego CA: Family Violence and Sexual Assault Institute.

We often block communication by using these kinds of responses:
(Put a mark by any of these that you have ever used with your partner)

1. ______ Ordering/directing/commanding

Don't talk about your mother like that.
Stop complaining.

2. ______ Warning/threatening

If you do that/you'll be sorry.
I can dish it out too/you know!

3. ______ Moralizing/preaching/shoulds

You shouldn't act like that.
A real man would never treat a woman like that.

4. ______ Advising/giving solutions

If you don't like it, you should just leave.

5. ______ Judging/criticizing/name-calling/labeling

You are so stupid that you never get anything right!
You will always be a loser.

6. ______ Reassuring/sympathizing/consoling

You'll feel different tomorrow.
Just forget it/it's no big deal.

7. ______ Interpreting/analyzing/diagnosing

This is because of your unresolved issues with your father.

8. ______ Sarcasm/Humor

Oh, you're going to start crying now?

Take a minute to think about the ones you have checked off. Is it possible that the use of these has messed up communication with someone important in your life?

SESSION 12 HOMEWORK #1

Handout (page 75 in *Handouts & Homework*)

Record three examples of your Active Listening responses over the next week.

1. Situation:

You Said:

2. Situation:

You Said:

3. Situation:

You Said:

SESSION 12 HOMEWORK #2

Handout (page 76 in *Handouts & Homework*)

Also: Fill out the questionnaire below on the Love Languages Personal Profile in preparation for the next group session!

1. Go the web page for the Love Languages® Quiz at 5 Love Languages (https://www.5lovelanguages.com/profile/couples/).
2. Fill out the information to get started on the quiz.
3. Complete this quiz online (should take 5–10 minutes).
4. Print results indicating your Love Languages Personal Profile and bring it with you to the next group session.

Session 13

THE FIVE LOVE LANGUAGES

Materials:

The Five Love Languages
Video: *The Break-Up* (starts at 18:50 with "All right guys, bye-bye" and ends at 24:35 after man walks out the door)
Love Languages Personal Profile (from previous session)

Program:

1. Ask each group member to report one gratitude (p. 59).
2. Focus on the mindfulness exercise (p. 60) for one minute.
3. Review the homework from the previous week.
4. Review the Weekly Check-Ins and use these to help guide the group discussion.
5. Read through the Five Love Languages handout together in group.
6. Play video: *The Break-Up*. Help the group identify the range of love language issues that show up here. Here are some of the obvious ones:
   a. RECEIVING GIFTS:
      - She wanted flowers.

   b. ACTS OF SERVICE:
      - She wanted his help with the dishes.
      - He believed that he really helped her by buying the lemons and by being a good sport during the family dinner.

   c. WORDS OF AFFIRMATION:
      - He really wanted appreciation from her about how hard he was working and how much he tried to make her happy.

   d. QUALITY TIME:
      - She complained that they never spent time together except for the things that he wanted to do (like the Michigan football game).

7. Review the results from each group member from their Love Languages Personal Profile (**NOTE:** This should have been filled out as homework prior to this group session). Discuss ways in which the results make sense to them or surprise them. Ask them to guess what the results will be for their partners.
8. If there is time, review the Communication Roadblocks handout—the "Anti–Love Languages."
9. **IMPORTANT:** At the end of this session, make sure to prepare the group members for the Husbands and Partners group session next week:

Next week is a special theme, called the Husbands and Partners group. As soon as you walk in the door, you will take on the role of your husband or partner, either current or the partner that you were with when this incident happened. You're all going to spend the whole group session, in character, as your partner. We've heard a lot about what's happened in your family from your point of view. Now we'd like to hear exactly how your partner feels and felt and what he or she goes through and went through. You'll be surprised how much you will learn!

TO FOCUS ON ALCOHOL AND DRUG ISSUES . . .

1. Discuss how much more difficult it is to stay focused on your partner's love language when you are intoxicated.

THE FIVE LOVE LANGUAGES

Handout (page 77 in *Handouts & Homework*)

Adapted with permission from Chapman, G. (2015). The 5 Love Languages®: The secret to love that lasts. Chicago: Northfield Publishing.

1. If you really love someone, you find a way to love that person the way he really wants to be loved.
2. Sometimes (often!) love languages are mismatched. This does not have to be a major problem—as long as you recognize your partner's language and try to speak to him in that language. And, when you feel like you are not being loved, remember that your partner may be showing love in a different language.
3. As you think about these love languages, remember that you are identifying what is most important to you. You are *not* evaluating your partner's performance.

Physical Touch

This language isn't all about the bedroom. A person whose primary language is Physical Touch is, not surprisingly, very touchy. Hugs, pats on the back, holding hands, and thoughtful touches on the arm, shoulder, or face—they can all be ways to show excitement, concern, care, and love. Physical presence and accessibility are crucial, while neglect or abuse can be unforgivable and destructive. Physical touch fosters a sense of security and belonging in any relationship.

Quality Time

For Quality Time people, nothing says "I love you" like full, undivided attention. Being there for this type of person is critical, but really being there—with the TV off, fork and knife down, not texting, and all chores and tasks on standby—makes your significant other feel truly special and loved. Distractions, postponed dates, or the failure to listen can be especially hurtful. Quality Time also means sharing quality conversation and quality activities.

Words of Affirmation

Actions don't always speak louder than words. If this is your love language, unsolicited compliments mean the world to you. Hearing the words "I love you" is important—hearing the reasons behind that love sends your spirits skyward. Insults can leave you shattered and are not easily forgotten. Kind, encouraging, and positive words are truly life-giving.

Acts of Service

Can vacuuming the floors really be an expression of love? Absolutely! Anything you do to ease the burden of responsibilities weighing on an Acts of Service person will speak volumes. The words he or she most wants to hear are "Let me do that for you." Laziness, broken commitments, and making more work for them tell them that their feelings don't matter. Finding ways to serve speaks loud and clear.

Receiving Gifts

Don't mistake this love language for materialism; the receiver of gifts thrives on the love, thoughtfulness, and effort behind the gift. If you speak this language, the perfect gift or gesture shows that you are known, you are cared for, and you are prized above whatever was sacrificed to bring the gift to you. A missed birthday, anniversary, or a hasty, thoughtless gift would be disastrous—so would the absence of everyday gestures. Gifts are visual representations of love.

SESSION 13 HOMEWORK

Handout (page 79 in *Handouts & Homework*)

Now fill out the Love Languages Quiz—this time from the perspective of your partner (or most recent partner). One way to do this is for your partner to actually fill it out, then discuss the results together. Or, if that is not possible, just fill this out as you believe your partner would answer it.

1. Go the web page for the Love Languages® Quiz at 5 Love Languages (https://www.5lovelanguages.com/profile/couples/).

2. Fill out the information to get started on the quiz.

3. Complete this quiz online (should take 5–10 minutes).

4. Print results indicating your Love Languages Personal Profile and bring it with you to the next group session.

Session 14

FOUR HORSEMEN OF THE APOCALYPSE

Materials:

Four Horsemen of the Apocalypse
Video: *Four Horsemen of the Apocalypse* (https://www.youtube.com/watch?v=1o30Ps-_8is)
Emotional Abuse and Mind Games
Conflict With Respect

Program:

1. Ask each group member to report one gratitude (p. 59).
2. Focus on the mindfulness exercise (p. 60) for one minute.
3. Review the homework from the previous week.
4. Review the Weekly Check-Ins and use these to help guide the group discussion.
5. Research by Dr. John Gottman and his colleagues (Gottman, 2000) has helped us understand patterns in marital communication that are almost sure to doom a marriage. The Four Horsemen of the Apocalypse handout explains the basic principles and examples of these communication patterns. Use the handout as a discussion guide for understanding how this works. Ask the women to identify themselves and their partners in these examples.

   Make sure to (1) identify the self-talk patterns that govern these patterns and (2) role-play alternatives for how to use different self-talk and different communications.

   Clearly highlight the following two main points:

   a. Review the definitions of the Four Horsemen of the Apocalypse. Emphasize that the women should be able to identify these patterns and to try and reduce them in their relationships.
   b. Discuss how the narratives that people have in relationships determine their emotional and behavioral reactions.

6. Play the video *Four Horsemen of the Apocalypse* to further explain the categories, and discuss.
7. Review the Conflict With Respect model (especially the softened start-up rules) and role-play examples of each, including the wrong way of doing it. Use this session to review many of the communication principles the group has already learned.
8. IMPORTANT: Make sure group members know to fill out the Which Attachment Style Am I? questionnaire as part of their homework in preparation for the next session.

TO FOCUS ON ALCOHOL AND DRUG ISSUES . . .

1. Discuss how substance abuse can increase the presence of the Four Horsemen of the Apocalypse.
2. Identify ways in which intoxication and patterns of abuse can interfere with the ability to manage conflicts effectively and to stay respectful of one's partner.

FOUR HORSEMEN OF THE APOCALYPSE

Handout (page 80 in *Handouts & Homework*)

ACCUSATIONS (CRITICISM)

Complaints are expressed in a destructive manner, as an attack on the other person's character: *You're so thoughtless and self-centered!*

In a constructive complaint, the person states specifically what is upsetting her, and constructively criticizes the other person's action, not the person himself, saying how it made her feel.

CONTEMPT (DISGUST)

Contempt is usually expressed not just in the words themselves but also in a tone of voice and an angry expression. Rolling the eyes. A look of disgust.

What distinguishes contempt is the intention to insult and psychologically abuse the other person. When contempt begins to overwhelm the relationship, one person tends to forget entirely the other person's positive qualities, at least when feeling upset. She can't remember a single positive quality or act.

DEFENSIVENESS

Defensiveness is the fighting-back response. Here the person refuses to take in anything the other person is saying. It is one arm of the typical fight-or-flight response.

Defensiveness feels like an understandable reaction to feeling besieged—this is why it is so destructive. The victim doesn't see anything wrong with being defensive, even though this attitude escalates a conflict rather than leading to resolution. Defensive people *never* say, *Maybe you're right*, or *I see your point*, or *Yeah, I get it. I think I owe you an apology.*

STONEWALLING

Stonewalling is the ultimate defense. The stonewaller just goes blank and withdraws from the conversation. This sends a powerful message: icy distance, superiority, and distaste.

Don't confuse stonewalling with a time-out. A time-out communicates respect. The time-out message is that the person cares enough about the relationship to take special efforts not to cause any further damage. And there is a very clear contract that the discussion will continue at a future time.

EMOTIONAL ABUSE AND MIND GAMES

Handout (page 80 in *Handouts & Homework*)

As with physical abuse, repeated emotional abuse can have severe effects on the victim's sense of self and sense of reality. These mind games sometimes leave more lasting damage than physical abuse. The person on the receiving end—male or female—may question his or her reality, feel powerless, become overdependent, and so on. Here are some examples:

Coercion

- *I am going to kill myself if you leave me!*
- *I'm gonna take these kids right now and you'll never see them again!*
- *I'll get a doctor to say you're crazy and put you away!*

Put-Downs

- *You're just like your mother, a fat, brainless ass!*
- *You're just like your father, a lazy, bull-headed ass!*
- *My mother was right about you—you'll never amount to anything!*
- *How come a big, strong guy like you can't make more money around here?*
- *You're acting crazy.*
- *There you go again—crying like a big baby.*
- *Nobody's ever going to want you!*

Control

- *I want to know everywhere you've been in the last 24 hours!*
- *I know you go to that school just so you can try to pick up some girl!*
- *Your family just messes you up—I don't ever want you to talk to them again!*
- *You can't go out. I want you to stay right at home with me.*

Blaming

- *It's your fault my career is going nowhere.*
- *Nobody else has ever made me violent! You must be doing something to cause this!*

Entitlement

- *I don't care what you think about my gambling—it's my money and I'll do what I want!*
- *So what if I bought that car without discussing it with you?*

CONFLICT WITH RESPECT

Handout (page 82 in *Handouts & Homework*)

Arguments can be a useful way to solve problems, or they can be never-ending battles that can increase tension and the risk of abuse. The central theme here, as always, is respect. Can you offer your partner respect even when you're upset? The following guidelines can make a difference:

DANGEROUS: THE NEGATIVE START-UP

Why am I the only one who ever does any cleaning up around here!
It may seem true at the moment, but . . .

- it is an exaggeration of the truth.
- it does not honor the positive qualities of your partner.
- it is usually communicated in a hostile tone of voice.

INSTEAD: RULES FOR A SOFTENED START-UP

I know you've been really busy with the kids, but I could really use some help getting the kitchen cleaned up.

- *Be concise.*
- *In the initial start-up complaint sentence, complain but don't blame.*
- *Start with something positive.*
- *Make statements that start with "I" instead of "you."*
- *Describe what is happening, but don't evaluate or judge.*
- *Talk clearly about what you need.*
- *Be polite.*
- *Express appreciation.*
- *Don't store things up.*
- *Restate your feelings in terms of the more vulnerable emotions.*

HOW TO AVOID UNFAIR BEHAVIOR (DISRESPECT)

- *Do not use name-calling or put-downs.*
- *Do not drag up old wounds from the past.*
- *Stay on track; do not go off in different directions.*
- *Do not threaten or intimidate.*
- *Do not assume that you will either win or lose this argument.*

- *Do not save up all your gripes to dump on your partner all at once.*
- *Be careful of mind-reading self-talk. Don't assume the most negative things about your partner. ASK!*
- *Do not deny the facts. Come clean.*
- *Do not gloat over a victory in getting your way.*
- *Do not sulk, ignore, pout, withdraw, or give your partner the silent treatment.*

SESSION 14 HOMEWORK

Handout **(page 84 in *Handouts & Homework*)**

Practice the softened start-up three times. Record the results.

1. My softened start-up statement:

   Response from my partner:

2. My softened start-up statement:

   Response from my partner:

3. My softened start-up statement:

   Response from my partner:

Session 15

APOLOGIES

Materials:

The Art of Apologies
Classic Apology Mistakes

Program:

1. Ask each group member to report one gratitude (p. 59).
2. Focus on the mindfulness exercise (p. 60) for 1 minute.
3. Review the homework from the previous week.
4. Review the Weekly Check-Ins and use these to help guide the group discussion.
5. Discuss the importance of genuine apologies in close relationships. It is especially important to frame the act of apologizing as something a secure women can do without feeling like she is trying too hard to please someone else.
6. Review the Art of Apologies. Discuss each item thoroughly and review the possible exceptions to these principles.
7. Review Classic Apology Mistakes and discuss. Practice and role-play apologies.
8. Assign homework.

TO FOCUS ON ALCOHOL AND DRUG ISSUES . . .

1. Discuss the importance of making amends based on destructive behaviors resulting from substance abuse.

THE ART OF APOLOGIES

Handout (page 85 in *Handouts & Homework*)

Apologies grease the wheels of most successful relationships. The art of delivering a sincere and well-timed apology is one that all of us should be very skilled at.

The obvious trigger situation for an apology is when you realize that you have done something that has hurt someone you care about. Even if your action was not intended to hurt or you were not aware of how it would affect the other person, an apology is still in order.

To apologize successfully, you need to have a solid platform of self-worth to stand on in order to not collapse into shame. The more self-worth you have, the more you can handle the ego blow of offering an apology—because admitting mistakes does not make you a doomed or despicable person. Just an imperfect one.

An effective apology requires four distinct elements to make it more likely to be well received (which is, after all, the point of the apology in the first place):

1. THE BASIC STATEMENT: "I'm sorry." No rationalizations, no excuses, no hedging. Just a simple statement that you are sorry and what you are sorry for having done. It could be big or very minor—it doesn't matter.

   Start by describing exactly what you did wrong, then just acknowledge that this was a mistake. Accept responsibility:

   - *I'm really sorry I started teasing you in front of your friends.*
   - *I feel terrible for having that affair and I am really, really sorry for how I have hurt you!*
   - *Sorry I forgot to make that bill payment.*

   Remember to get your *but* out of your apology: A *but* might sound like this: *I'm sorry I yelled at you, but you weren't listening to me*. Just stick with *I'm sorry I yelled at you.* Using *but* signals a rationalization, an excuse, and a focus on the other person's behaviors.

   While often your partner may have pieces to apologize for, a true apology only focuses on your behaviors. Take ownership of your part, find out how it impacted the other person, and begin to repair.

2. DEMONSTRATION OF EMPATHY: You need to make it as clear as possible that you really understand the pain or anxiety or mistrust that your actions have created in your partner: *I realize now how hurt you feel and how hard it is for you to trust me again. I get it now—or at least I'm trying to.*

   You need to make sure that you have listened to your partner's pain and that you clearly communicate the following message: *I want you to know that this is* not *going to slip out of my head.*

3. DEMONSTRATION OF INSIGHT: You need to offer the other person some evidence that you have learned something, or that there was some temporary circumstance that will not happen again, or at least that you will really be on guard against it the next time around:

   - *I think I was just feeling insecure, and this was some sort of way to make jokes and fit in! I won't let that happen again.*

- *There's no excuse—it had everything to do with me and feeling like I'm not getting enough attention. I wish there was some way I could go back in time and talk to you about what I've been going through instead of doing what I did!*
- *I was really rushing around last night, and I didn't pay attention. I'm going to start writing it in my appointment book to make sure I remember each month.*

"It's never enough to feel bad about an offense; **the hurt partner needs to hear reasons to feel safe in the future.**"—Steven Stosny, in Wachtel, E. (2019, March/April). Storm damage. *Psychotherapy Networker*, 61–64.

4. BEHAVIOR CHANGE: The proof is in the pudding. All the words and all the good intentions in the world don't mean a thing unless your partner sees, over time, that you have genuinely learned something from your mistake and that you are handling situations differently. Maybe not 100% perfectly, but definitely better. Remember that your partner cannot possibly feel secure until he or she has observed, over time, that you have changed. Obviously, the length of time that this takes is directly related to how serious the crime was.

CLASSIC APOLOGY MISTAKES

Handout (page 87 in *Handouts & Homework*)

1. Not being genuine. How do you like it when you hear *I'm sorry you feel that way* or *I'm sorry if that hurt your feelings*? Sometimes that might be okay, but most of the time this does not show sincere regret. In fact, it often makes your partner feel stupid for overreacting or being too sensitive. This usually does not get a passing grade as a genuine apology.

2. Crummy body language. Maybe the words are right, but there is no eye contact or even a hostile look. Or the tone of voice sounds sarcastic. This also fails the grade.

3. Waiting for the perfect moment. **It is never too late to apologize.** Some people wait for the perfect moment for an apology. This does not exist (although it's probably best not to do it in heavy traffic or when the baby is screaming). The perfect moment to apologize is the moment you realize you've done something wrong, or as soon as possible thereafter.

4. Getting defensive (see Nondefensive Listening below). Often we listen for the part of the criticisms or anger that we don't agree with, or some minor flaw in the person's story of what happened, or sometime when the other person treated us this way, or a reason the other person was oversensitive—anything to deflect from the simple responsibility of recognizing a mistake and apologizing for it.

5. Not listening carefully. Apologizing is much more than offering the words *I am sorry*. While these words mark the beginning, it is a process that can sometimes feel like a long-distance run. At the core of an honest and authentic apology is the ability to listen. You must be willing to sit with your partner's anger and pain. You need to stay there long enough to really grasp the injury and to validate the feelings.

6. Expecting immediate and total forgiveness. Remember Commandment 5: *We do not have control over any other person, but we do have control over ourselves*. All you can do is give it your best and most sincere shot. Your partner may never be able to forgive you, or at least it may take a while.

7. Apologizing too much. Some people apologize way too much, for the smallest things, or even when they haven't really done anything wrong. This is just plain irritating, and it's like crying wolf. The real and significant apologies will be weakened if trivial apologies distract attention from real issues.

SESSION 15 HOMEWORK #1

Handout (page 88 in *Handouts & Homework*)

Identify three apologies to offer to your partner or children. Make the apology and record the response from the other person. If you are not in contact with any of them, identify three apologies you would make if you had the opportunity.

---

1. Apology from you:

Response from partner or child:

---

2. Apology from you:

Response from partner or child:

---

3. Apology from you:

Response from partner or child:

SESSION 15 HOMEWORK #2

Handout (page 89 in *Handouts & Homework*)

Fill out the "Which Attachment Style Am I?" questionnaire below and score in preparation for next session:

WHICH ATTACHMENT STYLE AM I? **If TRUE, check white box. If FALSE, leave blank.**	**TRUE**		
	A	B	C
I often worry that my partner will stop loving me.			
I find it easy to be affectionate with my partner.			
I fear that once someone gets to know the real me, he/she won't like who I am.			
I find that I bounce back quickly after a breakup. It's weird how I can just put someone out of my mind.			
When I'm not involved in a relationship, I feel somewhat anxious and incomplete.			
I find it difficult to emotionally support my partner when he/she feels down.			
When my partner is away, I'm afraid that he/she might become interested in someone else.			
I feel comfortable depending on my romantic partner.			
My independence is more important to me than my relationships.			
I prefer not to share my innermost feelings with my partner.			
When I show my partner how I feel, I'm afraid he/she will not feel the same about me.			
I am generally satisfied with my romantic relationships.			
I don't feel the need to act out much in my romantic relationships.			
I think about my relationship a lot.			
I find it difficult to depend on a romantic partner.			
I tend to get very quickly attached to a romantic partner.			

WHICH ATTACHMENT STYLE AM I? **If TRUE, check white box. If FALSE, leave blank**	**TRUE**		
	A	B	C
I have little difficulty expressing my needs to my partner.			
I sometimes feel angry or annoyed with my partner without knowing why.			
I am very sensitive to my partner's moods.			
I believe most people are essentially honest and dependable.			
I prefer casual sex with uncommitted partners to intimate sex with one person.			
I'm comfortable sharing my personal thoughts and feelings with my partner.			
I worry that if my partner leaves me, I might never find someone else.			
It makes me nervous when my partner gets too close.			
During a conflict, I tend to impulsively do or say things I later regret, rather than being able to reason about things.			
An argument with my partner doesn't usually cause me to question our entire relationship.			
My partners often want me to be more intimate than I feel comfortable being.			
I worry that I am not attractive enough.			
Sometimes people see me as boring because I create little drama in a relationship.			
I miss my partner when we're apart, but then when we're together I feel the need to escape.			
When I disagree with someone, I feel comfortable expressing my feelings.			
I hate that other people depend on me.			
If I notice that someone I'm interested in is checking out other people, I don't let it faze me. I might feel a pang of jealousy, but it's fleeting.			
If I notice that someone I'm interested in is checking out other people, I feel relieved—it means that he/she's not looking to make things exclusive.			
If I notice that someone I'm interested in is checking out other people, it makes me feel depressed.			
If someone I've been dating begins to act cold and distant, I may wonder what's happened, but I know it's probably not about me.			

If someone I've been dating begins to act cold and distant, I'll probably be indifferent; I might even be relieved.			
If someone I've been dating begins to act cold and distant, I'll worry that I've done something wrong.			
If my partner was to break up with me, I'd try my best to show him/her what he/she is missing (a little jealousy can't hurt).			
If someone I've been dating for several months tells me they want to stop seeing me, I'd feel hurt at first, but I'd get over it.			
Sometimes when I get what I want in a relationship, I'm not sure what I want anymore.			
I won't have much of a problem staying in touch with my ex (strictly platonic)—after all, we have a lot in common.			

Add up all your checked boxes in Column A: ____ Column B: ____ Column C: ____
Scoring Key: The more statements that you check in a category, the more you will display characteristics of the corresponding attachment style.

Category A—Anxious:

- You love to be very close to your partner and have the capacity for great intimacy. You often fear, however, that your partner does not wish to be as close as you would like him to be.
- Relationships tend to consume a large part of your emotional energy.
- You tend to be very sensitive to small fluctuations in your partner's moods and actions, and you sometimes take his behavior too personally.
- You experience a lot of negative emotions within the relationship and get easily upset. As a result, you tend to act out and say things you later regret.
- If the other person provides a lot of security and reassurance, however, you are able to let go of your preoccupation and feel contented.

Category B—Secure:

- Being warm and loving in a relationship comes naturally to you.
- You enjoy being intimate without becoming overly worried about your relationships. You take things in stride when it comes to romance and don't get easily upset over relationship matters.
- You effectively communicate your needs and feelings to your partner and are strong at reading his emotional cues and responding to them.
- You share your successes and problems with your partner, and you are able to be there in times of need.

Category C—Avoidant:

- It is very important for you to maintain your independence and self-sufficiency, and you often prefer autonomy to intimate relationships.
- Even though you do want to be close to others, you feel uncomfortable with too much closeness and tend to keep your partner at arm's length.
- You don't spend much time worrying about your romantic relationships or about being rejected.
- You tend not to open up to your partner, and he often complains that you are emotionally distant.
- In relationships, you are often on high alert for any signs of control or impingement on your territory by your partner.

Session 16

YOUR ATTACHMENT STYLE

Materials:

Which Attachment Style Am I? (from previous session homework)
Video: *In Treatment*, Season 1 (HBO series), Jake and Amy—Week One (begins just before wife walks up to the door at 6:20 and ends after husband makes comment about her hemorrhoids at 16:23)
Can I Count On You?
Secure Communication

Program:

1. Ask each group member to report one gratitude (p. 59).
2. Focus on the mindfulness exercise (p. 60) for one minute.
3. Review the homework from the previous week.
4. Review the Weekly Check-Ins and use these to help guide the group discussion.
5. Review results from Which Attachment Style Am I? (completed in advance). Discuss the different attachment styles and how these show up in relationship issues.
6. Play video: *In Treatment*. Focus the discussion on the ways that the man has an insecure attachment (preoccupied/anxious) and how the woman has her own version (dismissing/avoidant). See if the group members can identify themselves in these roles.
7. Review the Can I Count On You? handout. Discuss which issues they recognize in themselves and/or in their partners.
8. Then review the Secure Communication handout for guidelines about effective responses.

TO FOCUS ON ALCOHOL AND DRUG ISSUES . . .

1. Discuss how attachment insecurity and fears can become activated when someone is intoxicated.
2. Discuss how much more challenging it to use effective communication skills when you are intoxicated.

CAN I COUNT ON YOU?

Handout (page 93 in *Handouts & Homework*)

Everyone walks around with doubts and insecurities about their intimate relationships. Here's a list of typical worries that people carry around. Can you count on positive answers to these questions in your relationship? Can your partner count on positive answers about you?

- *Will I be physically safe?*
- *Do I really matter to you enough that you'll put me first when it really counts—before your job, before your friends, even before your family?*
- *Can I count on you to give me space when I need it?*
- *Do I have to worry about you abandoning me?*
- *Do I have to worry about competing with someone else?*
- *Can I trust you not to hurt or humiliate me?*
- *Do I have to worry about your threats?*
- *Can I count on the fact that I really know you?*
- *Are you really paying attention to who I am and not who you imagine or want me to be? Can I be myself with you?*
- *Can I count on you to really act like an adult?*
- *Do you really value me, cherish me? Can I count on you to consistently let me know how important I am to you?*

SECURE COMMUNICATION

Handout (page 94 in *Handouts & Homework*)

SITUATION	INSECURE ATTACHMENT RESPONSE	EFFECTIVE COMMUNICATION
He's very busy at work and you hardly get to see him.	Call him every couple of hours to make sure you're on his mind.	Tell him you miss him and are having a hard time adjusting to his new work schedule, even though you understand that it's temporary.
He doesn't really listen to you when you're talking, which makes you feel unimportant and misunderstood.	Get up in the middle of the conversation and go to another room (hoping he will follow you and apologize).	Make it clear that it's not enough that he listens without responding. Emphasize that you value his opinion above anyone's and it's important to you to know what he thinks.
She talks about her ex-girlfriend, which makes you feel insecure.	Tell her it's pathetic that he's still talking about her ex, or . . . Bring up other women you went out with to let her know how bad it feels.	Let her know that conversations about her ex make you feel inadequate and unsure of where you stand, that you need to feel secure in order to be happy with someone.
He always changes plans at the last minute.	Do the same thing to him so eventually he'll learn how it feels.	Explain that you feel unsettled not being able to count on plans with him and that it's better for you to at least have a ballpark schedule most of the time.

It's important to remember that even with effective communication, some problems won't be solved immediately. What's vital is your partner's response—whether he is concerned about your well-being, has your best interest in mind, and is willing to work on things.

From Levine, A., & Heller, R. (2010). Attached. London: Rodale.

SESSION 16 HOMEWORK

Handout (page 95 in *Handouts & Homework*)

Now fill out the Which Attachment Style Am I? questionnaire—this time from the perspective of your partner (or most recent partner). One way is for your partner to actually fill it out, then discuss the results together. Or, if that is not possible, just fill this out as you believe your partner would answer it. See if it helps you understand your partner better and why certain situations activate your partner's fears.

WHICH ATTACHMENT STYLE AM I? **If TRUE, check white box. If FALSE, leave blank.**	**TRUE**		
	A	B	C
I often worry that my partner will stop loving me.			
I find it easy to be affectionate with my partner.			
I fear that once someone gets to know the real me, he/she won't like who I am.			
I find that I bounce back quickly after a breakup. It's weird how I can just put someone out of my mind.			
When I'm not involved in a relationship, I feel somewhat anxious and incomplete.			
I find it difficult to emotionally support my partner when he/she feels down.			
When my partner is away, I'm afraid that he/she might become interested in someone else.			
I feel comfortable depending on my romantic partner.			
My independence is more important to me than my relationships.			
I prefer not to share my innermost feelings with my partner.			
When I show my partner how I feel, I'm afraid he/she will not feel the same about me.			
I am generally satisfied with my romantic relationships.			
I don't feel the need to act out much in my romantic relationships.			
I think about my relationship a lot.			
I find it difficult to depend on a romantic partner.			
I tend to get very quickly attached to a romantic partner.			

WHICH ATTACHMENT STYLE AM I? **If TRUE, check white box. If FALSE, leave blank**	**TRUE**		
	A	B	C
I have little difficulty expressing my needs to my partner.			
I sometimes feel angry or annoyed with my partner without knowing why.			
I am very sensitive to my partner's moods.			
I believe most people are essentially honest and dependable.			
I prefer casual sex with uncommitted partners to intimate sex with one person.			
I'm comfortable sharing my personal thoughts and feelings with my partner.			
I worry that if my partner leaves me, I might never find someone else.			
It makes me nervous when my partner gets too close.			
During a conflict, I tend to impulsively do or say things I later regret, rather than being able to reason about things.			
An argument with my partner doesn't usually cause me to question our entire relationship.			
My partners often want me to be more intimate than I feel comfortable being.			
I worry that I am not attractive enough.			
Sometimes people see me as boring because I create little drama in a relationship.			
I miss my partner when we're apart, but then when we're together I feel the need to escape.			
When I disagree with someone, I feel comfortable expressing my feelings.			
I hate that other people depend on me.			
If I notice that someone I'm interested in is checking out other people, I don't let it faze me. I might feel a pang of jealousy, but it's fleeting.			
If I notice that someone I'm interested in is checking out other people, I feel relieved—it means that he/she's not looking to make things exclusive.			
If I notice that someone I'm interested in is checking out other people, it makes me feel depressed.			
If someone I've been dating begins to act cold and distant, I may wonder what's happened, but I know it's probably not about me.			
If someone I've been dating begins to act cold and distant, I'll probably be indifferent; I might even be relieved.			

If someone I've been dating begins to act cold and distant, I'll worry that I've done something wrong.			
If my partner was to break up with me, I'd try my best to show him/her what he/she is missing (a little jealousy can't hurt).			
If someone I've been dating for several months tells me they want to stop seeing me, I'd feel hurt at first, but I'd get over it.			
Sometimes when I get what I want in a relationship, I'm not sure what I want anymore.			
I won't have much of a problem staying in touch with my ex (strictly platonic)—after all, we have a lot in common.			

Add up all your checked boxes in Column A: ____ Column B: ____ Column C: ____
Scoring Key: The more statements that you check in a category, the more you will display characteristics of the corresponding attachment style.

Category A—Anxious:

- You love to be very close to your partner and have the capacity for great intimacy. You often fear, however, that your partner does not wish to be as close as you would like her to be.
- Relationships tend to consume a large part of your emotional energy.
- You tend to be very sensitive to small fluctuations in your partner's moods and actions, and you sometimes take her behavior too personally.
- You experience a lot of negative emotions within the relationship and get easily upset. As a result, you tend to act out and say things you later regret.
- If the other person provides a lot of security and reassurance, however, you are able to let go of your preoccupation and feel contented.

Category B—Secure:

- Being warm and loving in a relationship comes naturally to you.
- You enjoy being intimate without becoming overly worried about your relationships. You take things in stride when it comes to romance and don't get easily upset over relationship matters.
- You effectively communicate your needs and feelings to your partner and are strong at reading her emotional cues and responding to them.
- You share your successes and problems with your partner, and you are able to be there in times of need.

Category C—Avoidant:

- It is very important for you to maintain your independence and self-sufficiency and you often prefer autonomy to intimate relationships.

- Even though you do want to be close to others, you feel uncomfortable with too much closeness and tend to keep your partner at arm's length.
- You don't spend much time worrying about your romantic relationships or about being rejected.
- You tend not to open up to your partner and they often complain that you are emotionally distant.
- In relationships, you are often on high alert for any signs of control or impingement on your territory by your partner.

Session 17

THE RELATIONSHIP RESPECT CONTRACT

Materials:

Relationship Respect Contract
Contract Violations

Program:

1. Ask each group member to report one gratitude (p. 59).
2. Focus on the mindfulness exercise (p. 60) for one minute.
3. Review the homework from the previous week.
4. Review the Weekly Check-Ins and use these to help guide the group discussion.
5. Review the Relationship Respect Contract. Explain that a successful and healthy relationship depends on both partners feeling safe and secure. We can't guarantee that people who live by these guidelines will be successful—but we can be almost certain that couples who do *not* live by these guidelines are doomed to failure.

   Most of the items on the Relationship Respect Contract are self-explanatory. A few sometimes need a little clarification:
   - #4: This means trying to physically control the other person, by grabbing them, taking away car keys, blocking their path, and so on. The obvious exception would be if the partner is a danger to self or others (e.g., they are about to get behind the wheel despite being dangerously intoxicated).
   - #6: This refers to threats of abandonment ("Fine, if you don't want me, I'll find somebody else"; "I'm not going to live with someone who does this"; "You better get used to living on your own," etc.). These are weapons people use to hurt, scare, or retaliate—and they usually don't really mean it an hour later. These activate deep insecurities in the partner and often lead not only to distress but to unregulated responses.

     This is different than just setting a reasonable boundary, like, "If you don't get help with your drug addiction, I won't be staying with you" or "You have to stop cheating on me or I will leave." These are just clear statement of reality.

- #8: The exception to this would be if the couple has agreed to allow other sexual partners. Then sex outside the relationship is not really an act of infidelity.
- #9: Note that this does not state that there should be no use of alcohol or drugs, just no abuse.

6. Next, review Contract Violations. Go around the room and have each group member weigh in on the history of violations in their relationship, item by item. There will not be enough time to review everybody's response to every single item—which is fine, because they will complete this as homework.

TO FOCUS ON ALCOHOL AND DRUG ISSUES . . .

1. Identify ways in which intoxication and patterns of abuse can interfere with the ability to stick to the basic rules of respect in a relationship.

RELATIONSHIP RESPECT CONTRACT

Handout (page 99 in *Handouts & Homework*)

We recognize that our relationship will only have a chance to be successful if all of these guidelines are followed:

1. No incidents of direct physical abuse or violence.
2. No direct or implied threats of physical abuse or violence (to self, other, or property).
3. No direct or implied threats to behave in a way that would be extremely harmful to the other person (such as exposing personal secrets).
4. No physical restrictions on either party's freedom of movement.
5. No property destruction as an expression of aggression.
6. No threats to leave the relationship (except for temporary time-outs to defuse tension).
7. No pattern of extreme verbal put-downs, or character assassinations, or other humiliating acts.
8. No acts of infidelity or behaviors that suggest infidelity.
9. No pattern of lying or deception.
10. No pattern of abusing alcohol or drugs.

Other: ____

Both parties also agree to make all reasonable efforts to focus on building the positive aspects of the relationship rather than just complaining about the bad behavior of the other party.

______________________________________ ______________

Name Date

______________________________________ ______________

Name Date

CONTRACT VIOLATIONS

Handout (page 100 in *Handouts & Homework*)

Identify the ways this Relationship Respect Contract has been broken in the past, by you and by your partner.

CONTRACT ITEMS	VIOLATED IN PAST, SELF (YES/NO)?	VIOLATED IN PAST, PARTNER (YES/NO)?
1. No incidents of direct physical abuse or violence.		
2. No direct or implied threats of physical abuse or violence (to self, other, or property).		
3. No direct or implied threats to behave in a way that would be extremely harmful to the other person (such as exposing personal secrets).		
4. No physical restrictions on either party's freedom of movement.		
5. No property destruction as an expression of aggression.		
6. No threats to leave the relationship (except for temporary time-outs to defuse tension).		
7. No pattern of extreme verbal put-downs, or character assassinations, or other humiliating acts.		
8. No acts of infidelity or behaviors that suggest infidelity.		
9. No pattern of lying or deception.		
10. No pattern of abusing alcohol or drugs.		

SESSION 17 HOMEWORK

Handout (page 101 in *Handouts & Homework*)

Complete the Contract Violations chart below.

Then review the Relationship Respect Contract with your partner. Together, identify the ways this contract has been broken in the past, and see if you can both commit to at least *trying* to make sure the contract is honored by both parties in the future. IF YOU CAN, YOU SHOULD BOTH SIGN IT.

If you are no longer together or your partner is otherwise unavailable, write three additional items that you would include on your own personal Relationship Respect Contract for future relationships:

1.

2.

3.

CONTRACT ITEMS	VIOLATED IN PAST, SELF (YES/NO)?	VIOLATED IN PAST, PARTNER (YES/NO)?
1. No incidents of direct physical abuse or violence.		
2. No direct or implied threats of physical abuse or violence (to self, other, or property).		
3. No direct or implied threats to behave in a way that would be extremely harmful to the other person (such as exposing personal secrets).		
4. No physical restrictions on either party's freedom of movement.		

CONTRACT ITEMS	VIOLATED IN PAST, SELF (YES/NO)?	VIOLATED IN PAST, PARTNER (YES/NO)?
5. No property destruction as an expression of aggression.		
6. No threats to leave the relationship (except for temporary time-outs to defuse tension).		
7. No pattern of extreme verbal put-downs, or character assassinations, or other humiliating acts.		
8. No acts of infidelity or behaviors that suggest infidelity.		
9. No pattern of lying or deception.		
10. No pattern of abusing alcohol or drugs.		

Session 18

INTIMACY TRAINING: HUSBANDS AND PARTNERS GROUP

Materials:

Why Men Keep Their Mouths Shut About Domestic Violence
Video: *Men Don't Tell* (https://studio.youtube.com/video/F5d_6QCRX8c/edit)
Full DVD available from https://www.raredvds.biz/Men_Don_t_Tell_DVD_1993_Peter_Strauss_p/men_dont_tell.htm (also available on YouTube at https://www.youtube.com/watch?v=U_gLDF2dGLY)

- SESSION #3, Female projecting blame (begins at 28:12 and ends at 30:20 on DVD or 25:20–28:14 on YouTube)
- SESSION #15, Male keeping secrets (begins at 13:44 and ends at 16:11 on DVD or 14:18–16:47 on YouTube + 42:50–46:54 on DVD or 40:00–44:04 on YouTube)
- SESSION #23, Female taking responsibility (begins at 1:41:53 and ends at 1:45:31 on DVD or 1:27:50–1:31:53 on YouTube)

Program:

1. Ask each group member to report one gratitude (p. 59).
2. Focus on the mindfulness exercise (p. 60) for one minute.
3. Review the homework from the previous week.
4. Review the Weekly Check-Ins and use these to help guide the group discussion (in this group, information on the Weekly Check-In will be reported from the point of view of the partner).
5. Initiate the Husbands and Partners group. Many of the women in our groups have deficits in empathy. Their behavior might be quite different if they were genuinely aware of their effect on the other people around them. You might consider saying something like this as an introduction to this session: *The reason that you are each here is because, at some point in the past, you have done something that felt hurtful to your husband or partner. We all have. At the time, you simply may not have been aware*

of how you were affecting him, or what it must have been like to be in that position. We'd like to help you gain more of that knowledge, so that the next time around you'll be better informed. If you knew then what you know now (or what you are now learning), you might have made other choices.

a. The instructions are quite simple: *This is the Husbands and Partners group. We have invited you all here today to hear your side of the story. We've heard a lot about what's happened in your family from your partner's point of view. Now we'd like to hear exactly how you felt and what you went through.* A group member describes an interpersonal conflict situation from the point of view of her partner. All the group members play the role of their own partner. The entire group (for at least one hour) is conducted in this role-playing fashion.
b. Each group member must describe exactly what her partner is thinking or feeling—without sarcasm, without editorial comments, without trying to make the partner look bad. The group should keep giving feedback until they think she has played the role just right and has **truly gotten into the other person's shoes**.
c. The goal here is not problem solving, but rather understanding. It is also important to remind the women that gaining an empathic point of view does not necessarily mean agreeing with the other person, but simply understanding what it must feel like to be that person.
d. One way to structure this exercise is to make notes on the board during the check-in process. These notes describe the partner's point of view in the argument. Then use these for the empathy training exercise. For example:

   – Michael is suspicious because another man has been calling me.
   – Dennis gets on my case about going off to work out at the gym.
   – Belinda always makes decisions about our money and budget.
   – Sean insisted on watching ESPN *Sports Center* even though he knew it was time for my show.

e. Encourage all the group members to join in with questions and discussion of their fellow husbands and partners.

6. Begin by reviewing Why Men Keep Their Mouths Shut About Domestic Violence, with group members in character as men (or women, if they are in a same-sex relationship).

7. Another way to get the discussion rolling is by asking these sample questions:

   – *What seems to trigger conflicts between the two of you? Kids? Money? Sex?*
   – *How does jealousy show up in this relationship?*
   – *What do you love most about each other?*
   – *If you have kids, how well do you work together as coparents?*
   – *Are you afraid of your partner?*
   – *How has your partner broken your trust? How have you broken his or hers?*
   – *Do you think the two of you will make it?*

TO FOCUS ON ALCOHOL AND DRUG ISSUES . . .

1. Discuss how intoxication and patterns of abuse can interfere with the ability to understand where the other person is coming from.
2. In the homework assignment, instruct the group members to include substance abuse patterns in their essay.

WHY MEN KEEP THEIR MOUTHS SHUT ABOUT DOMESTIC VIOLENCE

Handout (page 103 in *Handouts & Homework*)

1. Men are afraid of being identified as a wimp and being ridiculed:

   Your GIRLFRIEND did this to you?? What's wrong with you?

2. Just like women, men don't want to face shame from others:

   Why did you pick a partner like that? What's wrong with you?
   Why did you put up with this for so long? What's wrong with you?

3. Men are afraid they will be identified as the cause of her violence:

   Come on, you MUST have done something to make her do this!

4. Men are not confident that they will be able to find community resources to support them: the police, court systems, or counselors might not believe them, shelters and victims' services for men are rarely available, and so on.

5. Just like women, men may fear that if they disclose the abuse or end the relationship, their partner might become more abusive and/or take the children.

6. And, just like women, abused men often don't report or leave because they still love their wives, they don't want to break up their family, they made a commitment to make the marriage work, they don't really want their partner to suffer the consequences and humiliation of the legal system—and they cannot tolerate the idea that they have somehow failed in their marriage.

SESSION 18 HOMEWORK

Handout **(page 104 in *Handouts & Homework*)**

Write one paragraph (at least 100 words) as if you are your husband or partner. The subject is "Sometimes I Don't Trust My Husband (or Partner) Because. . . "

Session 19

WHAT'S UP WITH SEX?

Materials:

Sexual Put-Downs and Mind Games
About Sex

Program:

1. Ask each group member to report one gratitude (p. 59).
2. Focus on the mindfulness exercise (p. 60) for one minute.
3. Review the homework from the previous week.
4. Review the Weekly Check-Ins and use these to help guide the group discussion.
5. Review Sexual Put-Downs and Mind Games. Refer back to the previous discussion on jealousy and misinterpretations; remind the women, through examples, how crucial their self-talk is when they encounter some form of sexual conflict in their relationships. Try to get through this pretty quickly, because the next exercise can stir lots of discussion.
6. Review About Sex and discuss. One of the best ways to do this is to go around the room, with each person answering one of the questions, then the next person answering the next question, and so on.

TO FOCUS ON ALCOHOL AND DRUG ISSUES . . .

1. Discuss the impact of drugs and alcohol on sex, including increased or decreased drive, increased selfish sexual behavior, lapses in judgment, and so on.

SEXUAL PUT-DOWNS AND MIND GAMES

Handout (page 105 in *Handouts & Homework*)

Sex can be, and should be, a wonderful aspect of a loving relationship. But often sexual messages are used in a way to hurt, retaliate, or control. If you can, try to be honest with yourself about which of these you may have used at some point in your relationships.

PUT-DOWNS

- Making jokes about men in your partner's presence
- Checking out other men in his presence
- Making sexual put-down jokes
- Comparing her body to other women or to pictures in magazines
- Criticizing his sexual performance
- Blaming your partner if you don't feel satisfied with sex

MIND GAMES

- Telling your partner that agreeing to sex is the only way they can prove they have been faithful or that they still love you
- Revealing intimate details about your partner to others
- Withholding sex and affection only to gain control over your partner
- Engaging in sexual affairs

GENDER PRESSURE

- *Real men should want it all the time.*
- *I owe sex to my partner whenever they want it.*

ABOUT SEX

Handout (page 106 in *Handouts & Homework*)

Adapted with permission from Koonin, M., Cabarcas, A., & Geffner, R. (2002). Women ending abusive/violent episodes respectfully (WEAVER) manual. San Diego CA: Family Violence and Sexual Assault Institute.

Sex has different meanings to each person. Some people view sex as a way to connect with another individual on a more intimate level. Some view sex as an extension of their love. Others may view sex as an outlet for stress and tension. The following is meant to help you clarify *your* definition of sex, and your values, feelings, and expectations when you are sexually intimate with someone.

I feel attractive to my partner when . . .

When my partner rejects me sexually, I (include feelings and actions) . . .

When I don't feel like being sexually intimate, I . . .

After having sex, I feel . . .

I think masturbation is . . .

A time I regret having sex (include why) . . .

A time I used sex to get what I wanted was . . .

I feel used sexually when . . .

Sex after an argument is . . .

Refusing sex to punish a partner is . . .

It is okay/not okay for me to cheat sexually on my partner because . . .

A person in a relationship should/should not flirt (include why) . . .

I think that men think sex is . . .

What I like most about sex with my partner is . . .

What I like least about sex with my partner is . . .

If I want to have sex and my partner doesn't, I usually . . .

SESSION 19 HOMEWORK

Handout (page 107 in *Handouts & Homework*)

Based on your own life experience, prepare three messages or words of advice you would want to pass on to your daughter about how to handle sex in a meaningful relationship.

1.

2.

3.

Session 20

EQUALITY, ROLES, AND DECISION MAKING

Materials:

Who Decides?
Rules and Roles: Spoken and Unspoken

Program:

1. Ask each group member to report one gratitude (p. 59).
2. Focus on the mindfulness exercise (p. 60) for one minute.
3. Review the homework from the previous week.
4. Review the Weekly Check-Ins and use these to help guide the group discussion.
5. Review the Who Decides? questionnaire and review responses in group discussion. Note that there are not always "correct" answers to these questions.
6. Review Rules and Roles: Spoken and Unspoken and discuss.

TO FOCUS ON ALCOHOL AND DRUG ISSUES . . .

1. Discuss how the rules and roles about appropriate use of alcohol or drugs can cause conflict in a relationship.
2. Identify ways in which intoxication and patterns of abuse can interfere with the ability to respectfully discuss decision making in a relationship.

WHO DECIDES?

Handout (page 108 in *Handouts & Homework*)

Adapted with permission from Pence, E., & Paymar, M. (1993). Education groups for men who batter: The Duluth model. New York: Springer.

Check below whether you think an item should be your decision, your partner's decision, or open to negotiation. Remember that there are no right or wrong answers here—as long as both partners agree about the decision-making process.

	Your decision	Mostly yours	Joint decision	Mostly your partner's	Partner's decision
1. Which friends can your partner spend time with?					
2. Which friends can you spend time with?					
3. Can your partner drink on certain occasions?					
4. Can you drink on certain occasions?					
5. Who decides on a sitter for the children?					
6. Will your partner get a job/go to school?					
7. Will you get a job/go to school?					

	Your decision	Mostly yours	Joint decision	Mostly your partner's	Partner's decision
8. How will your partner dress when he or she leaves the house?					
9. How will you dress when you leave the house?					
10. How will the children be disciplined?					
11. What is your paycheck spent on?					
12. What is your partner's paycheck spent on?					

RULES AND ROLES: SPOKEN AND UNSPOKEN

Handout (page 110 in *Handouts & Homework*)

Every relationship has rules and roles. When both people understand the rules—and agree to them—relationships work. When the rules are not clear—or when they are clear but violated—relationships suffer.

CATEGORY #1: DEAL-BREAKER RULES

These are rules that are usually clear to both parties, like . . .

- *It's not okay to cheat on me.*
- *I need you to be there for me when I am sick or distressed.*
- *It would be horrible if either of us tried to turn the kids against the other parent.*

CATEGORY #2: ASSUMED EXPECTATIONS

These are rules or expectations that we may have learned in our families or from previous relationships that we just assume everybody else would have, like . . .

- *Friday night is okay to spend with my friends, but Saturday night we always have to be together.*
- *We always have to eat dinner as a family.*
- *Christmas Eve is for a big dinner; Christmas Day is just for opening presents and hanging out.*

CATEGORY #3: RELATIONSHIP ROLES

These are expectations about the roles each of you are supposed to play in your relationship, like . . .

- *People should never raise their voice in a discussion.*
- *It's not okay for a man to cry.*
- *I need you to drop everything and talk to me when I need attention.*

SESSION 20 HOMEWORK

Handout (page 111 in *Handouts & Homework*)

Review the Rules and Roles handout. Based on these categories, identify one example of each category from your relationship:

1. What is one of the DEAL-BREAKER RULES or expectations in your relationship?

2. Now that you think about it, what is one of your ASSUMED RULES that you think *everybody* should understand?

3. What are some RELATIONSHIP ROLE issues that have been incompatible or caused conflict for you and your partner?

Session 21

KIDS WHO WITNESS

Materials:

Video: *First Impressions: Exposure to Violence and a Child's Developing Brain* (https://www.youtube.com/watch?v=eEEVKDW5NDc)
Video: *The Great Santini* (kitchen fighting scene begins at 1:28:29 and ends at 1:29:57)
Questions for Kids

Program:

1. Ask each group member to report one gratitude (p. 59).
2. Focus on the mindfulness exercise (p. 60) for one minute.
3. Review the homework from the previous week.
4. Review the Weekly Check-Ins and use these to help guide the group discussion.
5. Discuss the effects on kids of witnessing domestic violence. Begin by explaining that abusive fighting—verbal and physical—affects not only the adults, but also the children who witness it. Emphasize that children usually have excellent radar for tuning in to this behavior, even if the parents are sure it is all happening behind closed doors.
6. Play video: *First Impressions: Exposure to Violence and a Child's Developing Brain* and discuss.
7. Play video: *The Great Santini* and discuss. Review the ways in which each child has his or her own specific reaction to the violence. Identify self-talk for the children and the parents.
8. Review Questions for Kids. This next exercise is the most important component of this session. Any group member who has a child who has been exposed to the family violence will take on the role of that child. So you and the group need to know the age and name of that child. Usually there are at least a few group members who qualify.

If a group member does not have a child exposed, she should play the role of herself as a child if she witnessed family violence.

If a group member doesn't qualify for either of these roles, then she can just help the group discussion. The rest of the session is conducted with the women in character as the child, discussing their experiences, thoughts, and feelings.

The handout of Questions for Kids provides guidelines of questions to ask the "kids" to generate discussion. Review the self-talk and emotions. It is often helpful to have the "kids" talk to each other about what it has been like for them.

TO FOCUS ON ALCOHOL AND DRUG ISSUES . . .

1. Identify the role of alcohol in the violent scene from *The Great Santini*.
2. Discuss the following regarding the exposure of kids to substance abuse:
   a. Children are typically aware if a parent is abusing drugs and/or alcohol.
   b. Even young children are aware that certain substances that their parents ingest are special and alter their behavior in ways that most other things will not.
   c. While parents are engaging in substance abuse, children are often the victims of abuse and neglect.
   d. While parents are engaging in substance abuse, children are often forced to grow up too fast and take on adult responsibilities in order to make up for unavailable parents.
   e. Children are influenced by the rules that often exist in addicted families, such as keeping secrets. These often unspoken rules can lead to shame and guilt.

QUESTIONS FOR KIDS

Handout (page 112 in *Handouts & Homework*)

In this exercise, group members take turns role-playing, being the child in their house who has witnessed violence. Other group members interview these "kids" about their experiences.

1. What kinds of things do your mom and dad fight about?
2. What happens when your mom or dad gets angry or your parents fight? Can you describe any fights between your parents that you saw yourself? What did you see or hear during the fight? What was it like for you afterward (e.g., did you see your parents' injuries or the house torn apart)? What were your reactions?
3. What do you do if your parents push, shove, or hit each other? Do you leave the room or go outside?
4. Can you describe any fights between your parents in which you were caught in the middle, or when you tried to stop them? What happened?
5. Do they ever fight about you? How does this make you feel (scared, confused, sad, mad)?
6. Do you talk to anybody about this?
7. How do you handle your feelings since this has happened? Do you ever feel like hurting yourself or anyone else?
8. In an emergency for you or your parents, who would you call? Where could you go?

SESSION 21 HOMEWORK

Handout (page 113 in *Handouts & Homework*)

Complete the following Kid Stories exercise and bring it for group review next session.

1. You are an 8-year-old girl, and you really like playing video games more than anything else. Your dad has been getting drunk lately. He comes home and hits your mom, and he breaks things after he thinks the kids have gone to sleep. Your older sister has started using drugs and running away. One day after school, your mom says you're all going to be moving away from your dad, with her, to another town across the state, near your aunt and uncle. Your mom tells you that she can't trust your dad anymore and that you kids might be the next to get hurt. You've never seen your dad hit your sister, and he's never hit you.

   How would you feel when you heard about your mom's plans?

   How would you feel toward her?

   How would you feel toward your father?

2. You are a 10-year-old girl who's been really screwing up at school lately. Your dad is constantly on your case; it seems like nothing you do is right. You know your mom has been spending a lot of money, and he is always yelling at her about it. One time he locked her out of the house, and she had to stay outside in the rain until you snuck around the back to let her in. She yells right back at him, calling him bad names. Sometimes she even throws things at him and you can hear things breaking. You and your mom have left a couple of times for a few days, but she always comes back. It's hard for you to sleep. You want this to stop, and you ask if you can live with somebody else for a while.

   How would you feel toward your mother?

   How would you feel toward your father?

PART IX

PERSONAL RESPONSIBILITY

Session 22

ACCOUNTABILITY AND RESPONSIBILITY

Materials:

Video: *Sideways* (begins at 1:35:04 as car pulls into driveway, ends at 1:36:18 when man says, "Keep it elevated")
Accountability Assumption
Accountability Defenses
Video: *Blame and Accountability* (https://www.youtube.com/watch?v=RZWf2_2L2v8)
Accountability Statement

Program:

1. Ask each group member to report one gratitude (p. 59).
2. Focus on the mindfulness exercise (p. 60) for one minute.
3. Review the homework from the previous week.
4. Review the Weekly Check-Ins and use these to help guide the group discussion.
5. Review the Accountability Assumption handout.
6. Play the *Sideways* video. Here we have a spurned woman brutally assaulting the man who has betrayed her (in case it is not clear, she is hitting his face with her motorcycle helmet, not a purse). Discuss whether the group members believe that this justifies violence. It is particularly valuable to ask them to reverse the gender roles and see if this makes any difference.
7. Review the Accountability Defenses handout and spend some time discussing individual answers. Make sure that all group members clearly understand each of the defenses and specifically identify some of their own.
8. Play the *Blame and Accountability* video. Discuss how difficult it can be to take personal responsibility for our behavior and not blame others for what we do.
9. Introduce the Accountability Statement. Review each line carefully. Assist the women in filling out their own form using group discussion. In this structured discussion, each group member should be able to identify specific ways she has

acted destructively in her primary relationship. This is purposely structured so that *anyone* could identify incidents that would fit this description. We are hoping to create a nondefensive atmosphere in which the group members can openly recognize their abusive behaviors and clearly identify the ways in which—at that particular time—they justified the behaviors.

If you have background on the incident history, either from the women's previous reports or from previous documentation, it can be helpful to remind them of examples of behavior destructive to the relationship. This review is designed to give the women time to examine their behavior and self-talk and to generate group discussion about the rationalization process. Refer to Commandment #1 (*We are all 100% responsible for our own behavior*) throughout this discussion.

IMPORTANT: Make sure group members know to fill out the MAST questionnaire as part of their homework in preparation for the next session.

TO FOCUS ON ALCOHOL AND DRUG ISSUES . . .

1. When discussing accountability defenses, make sure to emphasize *I was drunk; what can I say?*
2. In the Accountability Statement, discuss the ways in which intoxication has been used to rationalize aggressive behavior.

ACCOUNTABILITY ASSUMPTION

Handout (page 114 in *Handouts & Homework*)

We are making an assumption here—that all of you want the best in your relationship and do not want to be in an abusive or destructive relationship. But something seems to come along and bring out behaviors in you that you thought you would never do.

We want to help you figure out what you have told yourself at those times when you have acted aggressively that somehow made it seem right or fair at the time.

When you figure this out, you become more powerful. And you become more fully accountable for your own actions. When you know what to look for, you are more likely to act like the woman you really want to be.

ACCOUNTABILITY DEFENSES

Handout (page 115 in *Handouts & Homework*)

Most people who behave destructively toward their partner find a way to justify it in their own minds. Even though they do not usually believe in being abusive toward a family member or partner, in certain situations they make an exception.

Then, afterward, they figure out some way to make it okay, rather than simply saying the obvious: I blew it. I crossed over a line, and it's nobody's fault but my own.

Here are some typical examples.

NO BIG DEAL: I wasn't violent; all I did was slap him.

INTENTION: I didn't mean to hurt him—I just wanted him to understand!

SELF-EXPRESSION: It was my turn to let him know what I've been going through!

INTOXICATION/LOSS OF CONTROL: I was drunk; what can I say?/I just flipped out; I didn't even know what I was doing.

PROJECTION OF BLAME: It's his fault; if he hadn't pushed me, or nagged me, or spent too much money . . .

ACCOUNTABILITY STATEMENT

Handout (page 116 in *Handouts & Homework*)

Adapted with permission from Pence, E., & Paymar, M. (1993). Education groups for men who batter: The Duluth model. New York: Springer.

To be accountable means to acknowledge and take responsibility for one's actions. This handout will help you acknowledge destructive behavior in relationships. Although such behavior does not always turn into physical abuse, practically everyone—in almost *all* emotionally intimate relationships—behaves destructively at times. This is an opportunity to recognize past mistakes and demonstrate a desire to change them.

As you fill out this form, remember Commandment #1: *We are all 100% responsible for our own actions*. You will not be turning this in, but we will use your response in discussion.

We are not asking you to admit to something that you did not do, or to take responsibility for something that someone else has done.

I have acted in the following destructive ways toward my partner. (Circle each)

Verbal Abuse		Controlling Partner		Intimidation		Mind Games	
Property Destruction		Manipulating Kids		Threats		Forced Sex	
Put-Downs		Stalking		Monitoring Mail/Phones		Sexual Put-Downs	
Isolation of Partner		Controlling Money		Ignoring/ Withdraw		Affairs	
Physical Restraint		Pushing		Slapping		Kicking	
Throwing Things		Choking		Use of Weapons		Other	

Other: ______________________________

- I take responsibility for these destructive behaviors. My behavior was not *caused* by my partner. I had a choice.
- I have used the following to rationalize my destructive behaviors in this relationship (e.g., alcohol, stress, anger, "he was criticizing me," etc.):

  1. ______________________________

  2. ______________________________

  3. ______________________________

- I recognize that my partner may be distrustful, intimidated, and fearful of me because of these behaviors.

SESSION 22 HOMEWORK #1

Handout **(page 117 in *Handouts & Homework*)**

Over the next week, pay attention to your self-talk and behaviors. Identify two examples in which you blamed someone else for your feelings or behaviors. You may use examples from the past if none occur to you this week.

1.

2.

SESSION 22 HOMEWORK #2

Handout (page 118 in *Handouts & Homework*)

Fill out the MAST questionnaire below and score in preparation for next session.

MICHIGAN ALCOHOL SCREENING TEST (MAST)

1. Do you feel like a normal drinker? ("normal" = drink as much as or less than most people)

Circle Answer: YES NO

2. Have you ever awakened the morning after some drinking the night before and found that you could not remember part of the evening?

Circle Answer: YES NO

3. Does any near relative or close friend ever worry or complain about your drinking?

Circle Answer: YES NO

4. Can you stop drinking without difficulty after one or two drinks?

Circle Answer: YES NO

5. Do you ever feel guilty about your drinking?

Circle Answer: YES NO

6. Have you ever attended a meeting of Alcoholics Anonymous (AA)?

Circle Answer: YES NO

7. Have you ever gotten into physical fights when drinking?

Circle Answer: YES NO

8. Has drinking ever created problems between you and a near relative or close friend?

Circle Answer: YES NO

9. Has any family member or close friend gone to anyone for help about your drinking?

Circle Answer: YES NO

10. Have you ever lost friends because of your drinking?

Circle Answer: YES NO

11. Have you ever gotten into trouble at work because of drinking?

Circle Answer: YES NO

12. Have you ever lost a job because of your drinking?

Circle Answer: YES NO

13. Have you ever neglected your obligations, your family, or your work for two or more days in a row because you were drinking?

Circle Answer: YES NO

14. Do you drink before noon fairly often?

Circle Answer: YES NO

15. Have you ever been told you have liver trouble such as cirrhosis?

Circle Answer: YES NO

16. After heavy drinking have you ever had delirium tremens (DTs), severe shaking, or visual or auditory (hearing) hallucinations?

Circle Answer: YES NO

17. Have you ever gone to anyone for help about your drinking?

Circle Answer: YES NO

18. Have you ever been hospitalized because of your drinking?

Circle Answer: YES NO

19. Has your drinking ever resulted in you being hospitalized in a psychiatric ward?

Circle Answer: YES NO

20. Have you ever gone to any doctor, social worker, clergyperson, or mental health clinic for help with any emotional problem in which drinking was part of the problem?

Circle Answer: YES NO

21. Have you been arrested more than once for driving under the influence of alcohol?

Circle Answer: YES NO

22. Have you ever been arrested, even for a few hours because of other behavior while drinking?

Circle Answer: YES NO

Please score one point if you answered the following:

1. No
2. Yes
3. Yes
4. No
5. Yes
6. Yes

7.–22. Yes

Add up the scores and compare to the following score card:

0–2 = No apparent problem
3–5 = Early or middle problem drinker
6 or more = Problem drinker

Session 23

I REALLY DIDN'T MEAN TO DO IT . . . I WAS DRUNK!

Materials:

I Really Didn't Mean to Do It . . . I Was Drunk
Video: *When a Man Loves a Woman* (starts at 30:54 gets out of the cab, ends at 35:40 after daughter tells father "Mommy died")
Why Do We Care? The Relationship Between Substance Abuse and Intimate Partner Violence
Why Do I Use?
MAST Questionnaire (from previous session homework)

Program:

1. Ask each group member to report one gratitude (p. 59).
2. Focus on the mindfulness exercise (p. 60) for one minute.
3. Review the homework from the previous week.
4. Review the Weekly Check-Ins and use these to help guide the group discussion.
5. Review I Really Didn't Mean to Do It . . . I Was Drunk and discuss.
6. Many people who hurt the ones they love have problems with alcohol. Some also have problems with other drugs, like pot and cocaine. It is unlikely, however, that alcohol and other drugs *directly* cause aggression. Rather, the causal connection appears to be indirect, acting through people's expectations, cultural norms, personality, mindset, and setting. And during withdrawal, the person may become irritable and liable to lash out. Long-term abuse may contribute to paranoia and aggression.

   Some people who are abusive have a true addiction to alcohol or other drugs. Anyone who has relatives who are alcoholic should be told to be particularly cautious about drinking. It may be best to abstain from alcohol entirely. Blackouts are one sign of severe alcohol abuse. The group members need to be made aware that, while drinking heavily, they may seriously hurt a loved one or a stranger and never remember the event. Society can still hold them responsible for their behavior while drunk, because they put themselves at risk by taking the first drink.

7. Play the *When a Man Loves a Woman* video. Even though this scene does not result in intimate partner violence, it does include violence to a loved one while under the influence. See of the women can recognize elements of this scene in their own lives and how alcohol and other drugs can alter their thinking, judgment, mood, and behavior. Emphasize their concern about the effects of their behavior on the people they love the most.
8. Review I Didn't Really Mean to Do It . . . I Was Drunk and discuss.
9. Review Why Do We Care? The Relationship Between Substance Abuse and Intimate Partner Violence and discuss.
10. Review Why Do I Use?
11. Review the MAST questionnaire (which should have been filled out as homework before the session) and discuss.

I REALLY DIDN'T MEAN TO DO IT . . . I WAS DRUNK

Handout (page 121 in *Handouts & Homework*)

Some people who hurt the ones they love have problems with alcohol. Some also have problems with other drugs, like pot, crack, and cocaine. Ours is a culture that often encourages the abuse of alcohol and the display of aggression under this influence. People under the influence sometimes do things impulsively they may not ordinarily do, and their judgment and control are impaired.

This session is about taking responsibility for all of your decisions and actions, including using substances.

People use chemicals for many different reasons. On the questionnaires that follow, think about the reasons you use alcohol or drugs. Then identify whether alcohol or other drugs impair your judgment or cause you to become aggressive.

And—ask yourself these questions as you think about the ways drugs or alcohol may be affecting your relationship problems:

- *Have you ever done something while under the influenced that you regretted afterward?*
- *Have you ever become more abusive or aggressive when using alcohol or drugs?*
- *Have you missed work/school due to your use?*
- *Have you made most of your bad choices while under the influence?*
- *Have you ever tried to cut back on your drinking or drug use?*
- *Has anyone ever been annoyed about your drinking or told you that you have a substance problem?*
- *Have you ever experienced memory lapses or blackouts?*

Any "yes" answers indicate that alcohol or drug use has probably impaired your ability to be fully in control of your life. Remember the 100% rule regarding responsibility. Alcohol and drug problems are usually progressive—without help, they get worse. Can you really be 100% committed to being in control of your life and still continue to abuse alcohol or drugs?

WHY DO WE CARE? THE RELATIONSHIP BETWEEN SUBSTANCE ABUSE AND INTIMATE PARTNER VIOLENCE

Handout (page 122 in *Handouts & Homework*)

- 60% of domestic violence incidents involve perpetrators who are drinking.
- The likelihood of aggression is eight times higher on days when the perpetrator was drinking alcohol.
- Binge drinking is tied especially closely with partner abuse. Binge drinking is defined as the consumption of five or more standard drinks in one sitting, at least once in the preceding 30 days. Individuals who engage in binge drinking are five times as likely to have interpersonal conflicts with their partner and engage in aggressive behavior.
- Alcohol intoxication can lead to negative feelings of depression, helplessness, and hopelessness. Being depressed significantly increases the likelihood of IPV.
- Over 50% of alcoholics have been violent to a partner in the year before beginning alcoholism treatment.

Information provided by Donald Meichenbaum, PhD.

WHY DO I USE?

Handout (page 123 in *Handouts & Homework*)

Think about the reasons that you use (or abuse) alcohol or other substances. Even if your use does not cause many problems in your life, it still serves some purpose. Check off on the list below the different reasons for your use of alcohol or other substances. We will discuss these in the next group session.

_____ To relax

_____ To feel more at ease in social situations

_____ Just because it tastes good

_____ Because my friends expect me to

_____ To have fun

_____ To avoid other people

_____ To feel more relaxed about having sex

_____ To avoid bad feelings (anger, depression, anxiety, loneliness, etc.)

_____ To have an excuse for getting rowdy

_____ To feel better about myself

_____ To stop worrying about problems

_____ To get a little buzzed

_____ To get really drunk

_____ To go to sleep

SESSION 23 HOMEWORK

Handout (page 124 in *Handouts & Homework*)

Describe one time when you really regretted something you said or did under the influence that has been damaging to your relationship or your family (100 words):

Session 24

STAKE IN CONFORMITY

Materials:

Stake in Conformity
Screw You!

Program:

1. Ask each group member to report one gratitude (p. 59).
2. Focus on the mindfulness exercise (p. 60) for one minute.
3. Review the homework from the previous week.
4. Review the Weekly Check-Ins and use these to help guide the group discussion.
5. Here is some background information about Stake in Conformity to explain to the group:

   "Stake in Conformity" means that all of us (who usually behave ourselves) put a governor on destructive or criminal behavior because we have a lot at stake for conforming. It usually pays off to be a good citizen, and there is usually a lot of cost for not being one.

   Most of us don't run red lights because if we did, the police would find us. We would have a big fine. It would hurt our insurance rating. It would cost us some money, and we would feel stupid. We have a lot at stake here.

   When you're in an argument with your partner and you're tempted to go off, or you're so frustrated with your kid, most of you do not just whack the person right across the face. Usually (we hope) that's because of empathy and anticipating how this other person whom you love would feel.

   But research and common sense tell us that it's also because you know you have so much at stake. Part of what stops you is knowing there will be a huge cost for this.

   Somewhere in your brain, most of the time, you are thinking like this: "I've got a lot at stake here. I do not want to lose my marriage. I do not want to lose my job. I do not want to go to jail. I do not want to lose access to my kids. I do not want to lose my standing in the community. I don't want to feel ashamed of myself.

I've got a lot at stake." The more you have at stake, the less likely you are to engage in abusive or criminal behavior.

6. Review Stake in Conformity. Review the answers to both parts of this handout. In this discussion, focus on the following:

   - Recognize extra risk for offenders who feel a low Stake in Conformity.
   - Anticipate the attitude, *What do I have to lose?*—see if the group can help identify what is of value to the person that will be lost.
   - Emphasize response cost, like, *Do you really want to lose something so valuable just because it* feels *like your partner (or somebody at work, or the court, or the system, etc.) deserves it?*
   - Create a positive vision of the future, including something to live for. For example, motherhood often serves as a signal to women that they have someone to live for, thus encouraging more healthy and responsible behaviors. Religion and a relationship with God can often provide an extra level of motivation to live according to the best possible values.

7. Review the Screw You! handout. Go through it slowly and dramatically. Discuss how valuable it is to use this kind of image in their heads to control their behavior—just at those moments when it seems impossible to control. This a dramatic example of Stake in Conformity.

8. Ask one group member to go through the steps in the homework, with the help of the group.

9. IMPORTANT: Make sure group members know to fill out the Safe at Home Questionnaire, Revised as part of their homework in preparation for the next session. **(Please note that the scoring of this is a little tricky. Group leaders should fill this out themselves first and practice the scoring, so they can more easily explain it to the group members.)**

TO FOCUS ON ALCOHOL AND DRUG ISSUES . . .

1. Discuss how tempting it is to turn to drugs and alcohol when you don't have much to lose in your life.

STAKE IN CONFORMITY

Handout (page 125 in *Handouts & Homework*)

One thing that stops people from crossing the line into violent behavior is a fear of losing something important.

But in order to fear loss, people must feel like they actually have something to lose. Research shows that arrest only works for people with something to lose by being arrested. People arrested for domestic violence with high levels of Stake in Conformity are less likely to assault their partners again after being arrested.

The higher your score, the greater the likelihood that you have a high Stake in Conformity and are less likely to commit any future acts of violence or aggression.

POTENTIAL LOSSES: How painful would it be if, because of your domestic violence, you (10 extremely painful, 0 not painful):

1. Lost your job ______
2. Lost your relationship ______
3. Lost access to your children ______
4. Served time in jail ______
5. Had to face your parents and other family members ______
6. Had to face your employer and coworkers ______
7. Had to face your friends ______
8. Had to face your church or religious group ______

SCREW YOU!

Handout (page 126 in *Handouts & Homework*)

Adapted with permission from Real, T., & Johnson, S. (2012). Confrontation in couples therapy—Who needs it? Psychotherapy Networker, 36(2), 46–61.

This is a description of a counseling session with a woman who described herself as a "rage-aholic." She would go off on her husband in wild verbal rages (never quite physical) in front of their kids, saying really insulting and damaging things that left everyone feeling wounded and scared.

She hated herself afterward and was seeking help to get more self-control. Here's how the counseling session went:

Counselor: *You have to stop doing this.*

She said, as most ragers do: *It comes upon me too quickly. I can't.*

Then the counselor made a strategic move: *Okay, here's what I want you to do. Do you have pictures of your kids?*

She got out her phone and showed him some pictures.

Counselor: *Okay, you have my permission to rage at your husband in front of your kids. But before you do that, I want you to look at some family photos of your kids and look into their eyes and say, "I know what I'm about to do is going to cause you deep and permanent harm, but right now, my anger is more important to me than you are, so screw you."*

He put his arm around her shoulder and said: *Let's practice that. Hold up the pictures, and say . . .*

She burst into tears: *I can't say that to my children.*

He said: *No, but you* are *saying that to your children. You're saying that each time you scream at their father in front of them. All I want you to do is say it out loud and own it.*

Then she said: *I'll never rage at my husband again for the rest of my life.*

SESSION 24 HOMEWORK #1

Handout (page 127 in *Handouts & Homework*)

Identify eight things that you stand to lose if you become abusive or violent with your partner again. The more of these you can come up with, the greater your Stake in Conformity.

1.

2.

3.

4.

5.

6.

7.

8.

SESSION 24 HOMEWORK #2

Handout (page 128 in *Handouts & Homework*)

Fill out the Safe at Home Questionnaire, Revised below and score in preparation for next session.

SAFE AT HOME QUESTIONNAIRE, REVISED

Instructions: Please circle the number that BEST describes how much you agree or disagree with each statement listed below.

ITEM #	ITEM STATEMENT	I Strongly Agree	I Agree	I Don't Agree or Disagree	I Disagree	I Strongly Disagree
1-C	The last time I lost control of myself, I realized that I have a problem.	1	2	3	4	5
2-M	I do not believe that I will return to my old ways of losing control.	1	2	3	4	5
3-P/A	I try to listen carefully to others so that I don't get into conflicts anymore.	1	2	3	4	5
4-C	It feels good to finally face how I've been messing up my life.	1	2	3	4	5
5-P	It's no big deal if I lose my temper from time to time.	1	2	3	4	5
6-P/A	I handle it safely when people get angry with me.	1	2	3	4	5
7-*	Sometimes I find that it is still very hard for me to avoid my old ways of treating my partner.	1	2	3	4	5
8-*	I have a problem with losing control of myself.	1	2	3	4	5
9-C	I want to do something about my problem with conflict.	1	2	3	4	5
10-C	I want help with my temper.	1	2	3	4	5
11-P	I'll come to groups but I won't talk.	1	2	3	4	5

ITEM #	ITEM STATEMENT	I Strongly Agree	I Agree	I Don't Agree or Disagree	I Disagree	I Strongly Disagree
12-P/A	I am actively keeping my cool when my partner(s) and I have conflicts.	1	2	3	4	5
13-C	I need to change before it's too late.	1	2	3	4	5
14-P	There's nothing wrong with the way I handle situations but I get into trouble for it anyway.	1	2	3	4	5
15-P/A	Even though I get angry I know ways to avoid losing control of myself.	1	2	3	4	5
16-M	I really am different now than I was when conflicts were a problem for me.	1	2	3	4	5
17-C	I guess I need help with the way I handle things.	1	2	3	4	5
18-P	It'll cost me plenty to get help.	1	2	3	4	5
19-M	I have been successful at keeping myself from going back to my old ways of acting when I have conflicts with my partner.	1	2	3	4	5
20-P	If my partner doesn't like the way I act, it's just too bad.	1	2	3	4	5
21-C	Some of what I see and hear about people being abusive seems to apply with me.	1	2	3	4	5
22-P/A	When I feel myself getting upset, I have ways to keep myself from getting into trouble.	1	2	3	4	5
23-C	I'm sick of screwing up my life.	1	2	3	4	5
24-M	I try to talk things out with others so that I don't get into conflicts anymore.	1	2	3	4	5
25-M	I am sure that I will never return to my old ways of treating my partner(s).	1	2	3	4	5
26-P	It's my partner's fault that I act this way.	1	2	3	4	5

27-*	It's okay that I got into trouble because it means that now I'm getting help.	1	2	3	4	5
28-P/A	It's becoming more natural for me to be in control of myself.	1	2	3	4	5
29-P	I'd get help if I had more free time.	1	2	3	4	5
30-P/A	I have a plan for what I do when I feel upset.	1	2	3	4	5
31-*	Recent changes that I have made probably won't last.	1	2	3	4	5
32-C	It's time for me to listen to people telling me that I need help.	1	2	3	4	5
33-M	I know the early cues for when I'm losing control.	1	2	3	4	5
34-P	I need to control my partner.	1	2	3	4	5
35-M	Anyone can talk about changing old ways of acting in relationships. I am actually doing it.	1	2	3	4	5

36. Please check the box for the description that best describes where you think you are, today, in your efforts to change the way you behave with your partner.

(Check only one box)

[ ] I am not really making any changes.

[ ] I am thinking about making changes in the future.

[ ] I am getting ready to make changes or I have made some changes already.

[ ] I have made some important changes and I have more to do.

[ ] I have made the changes I needed to make and now I have to keep up the good work.

SAFE AT HOME SCORE SHEET

NOTE: For each item, write your rating on the left underline and the Reverse Code on the underline to the right.

In other words, Reverse Code for 1 = 5, 2 = 4, 3 = 3, 4 = 2, 5 = 1.

Only the Reverse Code scores will be totaled at the end.

P = Precontemplation Stage
C = Contemplation Stage
P/A = Preparation/Action Stage
M = Maintenance

P **Reverse** ↓	**C** **Reverse** ↓	**P/A** **Reverse** ↓	**M** **Reverse** ↓
Item # 5 Score ___ ___	Item # 1 Score ___ ___	Item # 3 Score ___ ___	Item # 2 Score ___ ___
Item # 11 Score ___ ___	Item # 4 Score ___ ___	Item # 6 Score ___ ___	Item # 16 Score ___ ___
Item # 14 Score ___ ___	Item # 9 Score ___ ___	Item # 12 Score ___ ___	Item # 19 Score ___ ___
Item # 18 Score ___ ___	Item #10 Score ___ ___	Item # 15 Score ___ ___	Item # 24 Score ___ ___
Item # 20 Score ___ ___	Item #13 Score ___ ___	Item # 22 Score ___ ___	Item # 25 Score ___ ___
Item # 26 Score ___ ___	Item #17 Score ___ ___	Item # 28 Score ___ ___	Item # 33 Score ___ ___
Item # 29 Score ___ ___	Item #21 Score ___ ___	Item # 30 Score ___ ___	Item # 35 Score ___ ___
Item # 34 Score ___ ___	Item #23 Score ___ ___		
	Item #32 Score ___ ___		
Total: (REVERSE ONLY) ______ /8 = ___.______ **Average for P**	**Total:** (REVERSE ONLY) ______ /9 = ___.______ **Average for C**	**Total:** (REVERSE ONLY) ______ /7 = ___.______ **Average for P/A**	**Total:** (REVERSE ONLY) ______ /7 = ___.______ **Average for M**

SCORING: For each column, total the Reverse Code scores, then divide by the number listed in the rows above. You will end up with an average score for each column.

Precontemplation Stage (P): Client denies or minimizes having an anger/aggression problem and has no intention of changing.

Contemplation Stage (C): Client is thinking about changing but has no specific plans.

Preparation Stage (P/A): Client is preparing for change, or actually implementing a change strategy.

Maintenance (M): Client is sustaining the changes previously made.

The average score for each column reflects your scores on the categories above (Precontemplation, Contemplation, etc.)—but the only number that matters is the following:

Overall Readiness to Change: C _____ + P/A _____ – P _____ = _____

Mean Scores (Based on male and female domestic violence clients)

	Male	Female
P	20.37/8 = 2.55 (SD = 0.50)	19.40/8 = 2.43 (SD = 0.63)
C	34.16/9 = 3.80 (SD = 0.83)	34.65/9 = 3.85 (SD = 0.73)
P/A	28.36/7 = 4.05 (SD = 0.54)	29.47/7 = 4.21 (SD = 0.59)
M	28.66/7 = 4.09 (SD = 0.63)	29.50/7 = 4.21 (SD = 0.90)

Overall Readiness to Change

Male Average = **5.30** Female Average = **5.63**

This Overall Readiness to Change score measures how motivated you currently are to let go of aggressive attitudes and behaviors, learn alternatives, take responsibility, and grow as a person.

Scores above the mean indicate higher than average current Overall Readiness to Change.

Scores below the mean indicate lower than average current Overall Readiness to Change.

For more information: Sielski, C., Begun, A., & Hamel, J. (2015). Expanding knowledge concerning the Safe at Home instruments for assessing readiness-to-change among individuals in batterer treatment. Partner Abuse, 6(3), 255–272.

Session 25

FIVE STAGES OF CHANGE: WHERE ARE YOU AT?

Materials:

The Five Stages of Change
Safe at Home Questionnaire, Revised (from previous session homework)
Making Changes, Pros and Cons

Program:

1. Ask each group member to report one gratitude (p. 59).
2. Focus on the mindfulness exercise (p. 60) for one minute.
3. Review the homework from the previous week.
4. Review the Weekly Check-Ins and use these to help guide the group discussion.
5. Review the handout on the Five Stages of Change. Write the stages on the board and review examples. Make it clear that all group members enter the program at various different stages and that it is helpful to them and to us to identify their stage.
6. Now review the results from the Safe at Home Questionnaire, Revised that they filled out as homework. See if the test results match what they would have predicted—and if not, why not. Ask what would have to happen for them to move one stage further.
7. Review Making Changes, Pros and Cons. Go through this with one or more group members.

TO FOCUS ON ALCOHOL AND DRUG ISSUES . . .

1. Review the stages of change that someone is likely to go through as they try to stop drinking or using.

THE FIVE STAGES OF CHANGE

Handout (page 133 in *Handouts & Homework*)

Researchers have found that anyone who makes a successful decision to change something that is not working in his or her life goes through a series of stages. This is true for smoking, dieting, drugs and alcohol, gambling, aggressive behavior, and so on.

Everybody who comes into our program enters at their own stage of change. It helps us and it will help you to understand what your stage is—and to notice at various points in your program if there are any changes.

If you do notice movement in these stages, it is valuable to figure out how that happened. Usually something clicks—or the problems reach a breaking point and you decide you really have to move forward.

Here are the classic stages—maybe you can identify even more:

1: PRECONTEMPLATION

I don't have a problem with aggression—so I have no interest in changing my behavior.

2: CONTEMPLATION

I realize I might have a problem with aggression—but I'm not sure I want to do anything about it yet. Maybe later.

3 PREPARATION (or DETERMINATION)

I know now that I have a problem with aggression—and I have to do something about this so I can have a better life and better relationships.

4: ACTION

I realize now that my abusive behavior is unacceptable and I will not allow myself to return to it. I am committing myself to groups, therapy, spiritual guidance, books, and good people—anything to help me make these changes.

5: MAINTENANCE

I realize that it's going to take a lot of work, over a long period of time, to maintain these changes and keep growing. I have to surround myself with the right people and watch carefully for warning signs that I might be slipping.

MAKING CHANGES, PROS AND CONS

Handout (page 134 in *Handouts & Homework*)

Whenever we think about keeping an old behavior or changing it, it helps to weight the pros and cons—then come to an intelligent decision. Try this with your anger/aggression.

GOOD Things About Anger/Aggression	GOOD Things About Changing Anger/Aggression
NOT-GOOD Things About Anger/Aggression	NOT-GOOD Things About Changing Anger/Aggression

SESSION 25 HOMEWORK

Handout (page 135 in *Handouts & Homework*)

MAKING CHANGES, PROS AND CONS

If you did not do this in the group session, fill in the blanks on this chart about the pros and cons.

If you did this in the group, pick out another behavior and apply the model to that.

GOOD Things About Anger/Aggression	GOOD Things About Changing Anger/Aggression
NOT-GOOD Things About Anger/Aggression	NOT-GOOD Things About Changing Anger/Aggression

Session 26

THE PREVENTION PLAN

Materials:

The Prevention Plan

Program:

1. Ask each group member to report one gratitude (p. 59).
2. Focus on the mindfulness exercise (p. 60) for one minute.
3. Review the homework from the previous week.
4. Review the Weekly Check-Ins and use these to help guide the group discussion.
5. The following are sample instructions for implementing the Prevention Plan:

The first step is actually down at the bottom.

First you figure out the behavior that you do not want to do anymore, like "screaming at my husband in public." You want to make sure that you never *do that again, no matter what the circumstances of perceived provocation.*

Then, at the top, you have to figure out what would be the cue or trigger or red flag, what might put you in a zone where you will be really tempted to go off like that. It might be "seeing my husband talking with an attractive woman."

Then you move on to figuring out several different emergency strategies and interventions. The first we call the Scare Yourself. Picture the worst thing that is going to happen if you blow up. In treatment groups for domestic violence, the number one Scare Yourself image is usually something like this: I never want to be in a police station or behind bars ever again.

The second most common Scare Yourself image for most people has to do with kids—either losing kids or even something like this: I never want to see that look on my kids' faces again, them being ashamed or scared of me or their daddy. And of course sometimes it has to do with their partner: I never want to see him that scared of me again. I don't want to lose him.

The second tool or intervention is the Self-Talk, something you can say to yourself at those crisis moments that is going to keep you on track: I cannot afford to do this, or It's not worth it, or I know he didn't really mean what he just said. Something that you can put into your consciousness that will lower the arousal level just enough that you don't do something horrible and irrevocable. This does not mean something that would put a smile on your face—because almost by definition these situations will not allow for that.

Another strategy is Fun and Distraction, which just means doing something to distract yourself from the intensity of the anger and rage. This could be playing a video game or cleaning up the kitchen listening to music or working out or just taking a nap.

The final strategy, when possible, is called the Friend or Ally: somebody you can call or text or go hang with. The best friend or ally is someone who will help center you—could be your best friend, your mother, your sponsor, your brother, your minister, and so on. Obviously that person is not always available—but the Scare Yourself image and the Self-Talk are always available. Those take about half a second to activate, and they are completely internal. The other ones are behaviors which you may or may not have access to at that time, but that are still part of the overall prevention package.

6. In generating ideas for the Prevention Plan in the group, there are three principles to keep in mind:

   a. Be very specific about problem behavior:

GENERAL	SPECIFIC (Much better)
Losing my temper	*Pushing my son*
Blowing it	*Yelling at my coworker*

   b. Be very specific about trigger behavior:

GENERAL	SPECIFIC (Much better)
Feeling disrespected	*When my husband puts me down for not making enough money*

   c. Use input from other people who care about you (especially the group members—they are experts at this!) to help put together your Prevention Plan.

7. Go through the preparation of the Prevention Plan with as many group members as possible. Each one should take about 5 to 10 minutes. Since you will not usually have time to do one with everyone, use the more veteran members of the group who are closer to graduation. Note that *all* group members will need to prepare and present their own Prevention Plan at some point before completing the STOP Program.

TO FOCUS ON ALCOHOL AND DRUG ISSUES . . .

1. Discuss ways to apply the Prevention Plan to drug and alcohol issues.

THE PREVENTION PLAN

Handout (page 136 in *Handouts & Homework*)

Purpose: To prepare you for future situations when you might be tempted to behave destructively to yourself and/or others.

STEP 2, Cue or Trigger (What could set you off?):

STEP 3, Coping Strategies:

1. **SCARE YOURSELF IMAGE—Example:** Remember the damage to people you love, remember the consequences when you have made mistakes in the past, and so on. What scary image would have an impact on you?

2. **SELF-TALK—Example:** *This isn't worth it. Nobody's perfect. I want to keep my life together.* What would that be for you?

3. **RELAXATION/DISTRACTION—Example:** Deep breathing, listening to music, working out, cleaning up the kitchen, and so on. What would work for you?

4. **FRIENDS/ALLIES—Example:** Call a friend, crisis line, therapist, sponsor, or family member. Who would that be for you?

STEP 1, Behavior I Do *Not* Want to Do (be specific):

____

____

SESSION 26 HOMEWORK

Handout (page 137 in *Handouts & Homework*)

If you *did not* get the chance to work on the Prevention Plan in the group session, prepare one of your own.

If you *did* get the chance to work on the Prevention Plan in the group session, prepare one for another situation and behavior you want to manage.

PART X

EXIT SESSIONS

Exit Session I

MOST VIOLENT AND/OR MOST DISTURBING INCIDENT

THIS MATERIAL (AND THE MATERIAL FROM EXIT SESSION II) SHOULD BE PRESENTED ONLY WHEN A GROUP MEMBER IS NEAR THE END POINT OF THE TREATMENT PROGRAM. THEN THE REGULARLY SCHEDULED GROUP CONTENT SHOULD RESUME.

Program:

Here are the suggested instructions for this very important exercise for a group member who is close to terminating the group program:

Tell us, in detail, the most disturbing abusive incident in your relationship that you have committed. This is not necessarily the most physically injurious event or the one you got busted for, but rather the one that stands out as the most emotionally upsetting.

There may have been other more abusive incidents in your relationship committed by your partner—but this assignment is to choose a situation when you have behaved the most abusively toward him.

It is very important for you to describe this incident as vividly as possible, in detail, as if it were happening in slow motion. Each step of the way, we need to hear about your self-talk, your emotions, and your physical state.

(Note to the group leader: Particularly important is her affect. You may need to say repeatedly, "Describe how you are feeling at this point." The goal here is to diminish as much of the original denial and minimization as possible.)

We think you're ready for this now in ways that you were not when you first came into this program. This is an opportunity to go into more depth with these issues—particularly with some of the new skills and information that you now have.

We also want you to identify your partner's and child's self-talk, your partner's and child's emotions, and your partner's and child's physical states.

We know you can do this.

This should all be presented with some gravitas; the message should be that the group member is now ready, much more than when she began the program, to offer this information with the depth and respect it deserves.

If you determine that a group member does not present this information sufficiently or with seriousness (which happens occasionally), she is not allowed to graduate from the STOP Program.

Exit Session II

PREVENTION PLAN

Please note that *each* group member, in one of her final few sessions, must present her Prevention Plan (see Session 26 for instructions).

If you determine that a group member does not present this information sufficiently or with seriousness (which happens occasionally), she is not allowed to graduate from the STOP Program.

REFERENCES

Archer, J. (2000). Sex differences in aggression between heterosexual partners: A meta-analytic review. *Psychological Bulletin, 126*(5), 651–680.

Babcock, J. C., Miller, S. A., & Siard, C. (2003). Toward a typology of abusive women: Differences between partner-only and generally violent women in the use of violence. *Psychology of Women Quarterly, 27*(2), 153–161.

Barnett, O. W., Lee, C. Y., & Thelen, R. E. (1997). Gender differences in attributions of self-defense and control in interpartner aggression. *Violence Against Women, 3*(5), 462–481.

Bookwala, J., & Zdaniuk, B. (1998). Adult attachment styles and aggressive behavior within dating relationships. *Journal of Social and Personal Relationships, 15*(2), 175–190. doi:10.1177/0265407598152003

Bowen, E. L. (2008). *Domestic violence treatment for abusive women: A treatment manual.* New York: Routledge.

Caldwell, J. E., Swan, S. C., Allen, C. T., Sullivan, T. P., & Snow, D. L. (2009). Why I hit him: Women's reasons for intimate partner violence. *Journal of Aggression, Maltreatment and Trauma, 18*(7), 672–697. doi:10.1080/10926770903231783

Carney, M., Buttell, F., & Dutton, D. (2007). Women who perpetrate intimate partner violence: A review of the literature with recommendations for treatment. *Aggression and Violent Behavior, 12*(1), 108–115.

Carrado, M., George, M. J., Loxam, E., Jones, L., & Templar, D. (1996). Aggression in British heterosexual relationships: A descriptive analysis. *Aggressive Behavior, 22*, 401–415.

Cascardi, M., & Vivian, D. (1995). Context for specific episodes of marital violence: Gender and severity of violence differences. *Journal of Family Violence, 10*, 265–293.

Conradi, L., Geffner, R., Hamberger, L. K., & Lawson, G. (2009). An exploratory study of women as dominant aggressors of physical violence in their intimate relationships. *Journal of Aggression, Maltreatment and Trauma, 18* (7), 718–738. https://doi.org/10.1080/10926770903231718

Davis, K. E., Coker, A. L., & Sanderson, M. (2002). Physical and mental health effects of being stalked for men and women. *Violence and Victims, 17*(4), 429–443.

Dutton, D. G. (1995). *The domestic assault of women: Psychological and criminal justice perspectives.* Vancouver: University of British Columbia Press.

Dutton, D. G. (1998). *The abusive personality: Violence and control in intimate relationships.* New York: Guilford Press.

Dutton, D. G., Saunders, K., Starzomski, A., & Bartholomew, K. (1994). Intimacy-anger and insecure attachment as precursors of abuse in intimate relationships. *Journal of Applied Social Psychology, 24*(15), 1367–1386.

Dutton, D., van Ginkel, C., & Strazomski, A. (1995). The role of shame and guilt in the intergenerational transmission of abusiveness. *Violence and Victims, 10*(2), 121–131.

Ehlers, A., & Clark, D. M. (2000). A cognitive model of posttraumatic stress disorder. *Behavior Research and Therapy 38*, 319–345.

Elmquist, J., Hamel, J., Shorey, R. C., Labrecque, L., Ninnemann, A., & Stuart, G. L. (2014). Motivations for intimate partner violence in men and women arrested for domestic violence and court referred to batterer intervention programs. *Partner Abuse, 5*(4), 359–374.

Emmons, R. A. (2013). *Gratitude works! A 21-day program for creating emotional prosperity.* San Francisco: Jossey-Bass.

Erickson, M., & Rossi, E. (1979). *Hypnotherapy: An exploratory casebook.* New York: Irvington.

Felitti, V. J., Anda, R. F., Nordenberg, D., Williamson, D. F., Spitz, A. M., Edwards, V., Koss, M. P., & Marks, J. S. (1998). Relationship of childhood abuse and household dysfunction to many of the leading causes of death in adults: The Adverse Childhood Experiences (ACE) Study. *American Journal of Preventive Medicine, 14*, 245–258.

Fiebert, M. S., & Gonzalez, D. M. (1997). Women who initiate assaults: The reasons offered for such behavior. *Psychological Reports, 80*, 583–590.

Fischer, K. L., & McGrane, M. F. (1997). *Journey beyond abuse: A step-by-step guide to facilitating women's domestic abuse groups*. St. Paul: Amherst H. Wilder Foundation.

Follingstad, D. R., DeHart, D. D., & Green, E. P. (2004). Psychologists' judgments of psychologically aggressive actions when perpetrated by a husband versus a wife. *Violence and Victims, 19*(4), 435–452.

Follingstad, D. R., Wright, S., Lloyd, S., & Sebastian, J. A. (1991). Sex differences in motivations and effects in dating violence. *Family Relations, 40*, 51–57.

Foshee, V. A., Linder, F., & Rice, J. (2001). *Gender differences in adolescent dating violence profiles* [Paper presentation]. International Family Violence Research Conference, Portsmouth, NH.

Geffner, R., & Mantooth, C. (1995). *A psychoeducational model for ending wife/partner abuse: A program manual for treating individuals and couples*. Tyler, TX: Family Violence and Sexual Assault Institute.

Gilligan, S. (1987). *Therapeutic trances*. New York: Brunner/Mazel.

Goldenson, J., Geffner, R., Foster, S. L., & Clipson, C. R. (2007). Female domestic violence offenders: Their attachment security, trauma symptomatology and personality organization. *Violence and Victims, 22*, 530–543.

Gottman, J. (2000). *The seven principles for making marriage work*. New York: Three Rivers.

Hamberger, L. K., Lohr, J. M., Bonge, D., & Tolin, D. F. (1997). An empirical classification of motivations for domestic violence. *Violence Against Women, 3*, 401–423.

Hamberger, L. K., & Potente, T. (1994). Counseling heterosexual women arrested for domestic violence: Implications for theory and practice. *Violence and Victims, 9*, 125–137.

Harned, M. S. (2001). Abused women or abused men? An examination of the context and outcomes of dating violence. *Violence and Victims, 16*, 269–285.

Henderson, A. J. Z., Bartholomew, K., Trinke, S. J., & Kwong, M. J. (2005). When loving means hurting: An exploration of attachment and intimate abuse in a community sample. *Journal of Family Violence, 20*(4), 219–230. doi:10.1007/s10896-005-5985-y

Henning, K., & Holdford, R. (2006). Minimization, denial, and victim blaming by batterers: How much does the truth matter? *Criminal Justice and Behavior, 33*(1), 110–130. doi:10.1177/0093854805282322

Henning, K., Jones, A., & Holdford, R. (2003). Treatment needs of women arrested for domestic violence: A comparison with male offenders. *Journal of Interpersonal Violence, 18*(8), 839–856.

Hettrich, E. L., & O'Leary, K. D. (2007). Females' reasons for their physical aggression in dating relationships. *Journal of Interpersonal Violence, 22*(9), 1131–1143. doi:10.1177/0886260507303729

Johnson, M. P. (2008). *A typology of domestic violence: Intimate terrorism, violent resistance, and situational couple violence*. Northeastern Series on Gender, Crime, and Law. Holliston, MA: Northeastern.

Johnson, M., & Ferraro, K. (2000). Research on domestic violence in the 1990s: Making distinctions. *Journal of Marriage and the Family, 62*(4), 948–963.

Judicial Council of California Advisory Committee. (2014). *Jury Instructions: Additions and Revisions to Criminal Jury Instructions*. http://www.courts.ca.gov/documents/jc-20120228-itemA15.pdf

Katz, J., Kuffel, S., & Coblentz, A. (2002). Are there gender differences in sustaining dating violence? An examination of frequency, severity, and relationship satisfaction. *Violence and Victims, 17*, 247–271.

Koonin, M., Cabarcas, A., & Geffner, R. (2002). *Women ending abusive/violent episodes respectfully (WEAVER) manual*. San Diego: Family Violence and Sexual Assault Institute.

Korb, A. (2015). *The upward spiral: Using neuroscience to reverse the course of depression, one small change at a time*. Oakland, CA: New Harbinger.

Kurz, D. (1993). Physical assaults by husbands: A major social problem. In R. J. Gelles & D. R. Loseke (Eds.), *Current controversies on family violence* (pp. 88–103). Newbury Park, CA: Sage.

Langhinrichsen-Rohling, J., Misra, T. A., Selwyn, C., & Rohling, M. L. (2012). Rates of bi-directional versus uni-directional intimate partner violence across samples, sexual orientations, and race/ethnicities: A comprehensive review. *Partner Abuse, 3*(2), 199–230.

Langhinrichsen-Rohling, J., Neidig, P., & Thorn, G. (1995). Violent marriages: Gender differences in levels of current violence and past abuse. *Journal of Family Violence, 10*, 159–176.

Larance, L. Y., Cape, J. K., & Garvin, D. J. H. (2012). *Meridians for incarcerated women: Facilitators' manual.* Washtenaw County, MI: Catholic Social Services of Washtenaw County.

Larance, L. Y., Hoffman-Ruzicka, A., & Shivas, J. B. (2009). *Vista: A program for women who use force/curriculum guide.* Morristown, NJ: Jersey Center for Nonviolence.

Leisring, P. A., Dowd, L., & Rosenbaum, A. (2003). Treatment of partner aggressive women. *Journal of Aggression, Maltreatment and Trauma, 7*(1/2), 257–276.

Levine, A., & Heller, R. (2010). *Attached.* London: Rodale.

Margolies, L., & Leeder, E. (1995). Violence at the door: Treatment of lesbian batterers. *Violence Against Women, 1*(2), 139–157.

McNulty, J. K., & Hellmuth, J. C. (2008). Emotion regulation and intimate partner violence in newlyweds. *Journal of Family Psychology, 22*(5), 794–797.

Ménard, K. S., Hall, G. C., Phung, A. H., Ghebrial, M. E., & Martin, L. (2003). Gender differences in sexual harassment and coercion in college students: Developmental, individual, and situational determinants. *Journal of Interpersonal Violence, 18*(10), 1222–1239.

Miller, W. R., & Rollnick, S. (1991). *Motivational interviewing: Preparing people to change addictive behavior.* New York: Guilford.

Murphy, C. M., & O'Leary, K. D. (1989). Psychological aggression predicts physical aggression in early marriage. *Journal of Consulting and Clinical Psychology, 57*(5), 579–582.

O'Hanlon, W., & Weiner-Davis, M. (1989). *In search of solutions.* New York: Norton.

O'Sullivan, L. F., Byers, S. E., & Finkelman, L. (1998). A comparison of male and female college students' experiences of sexual coercion. *Psychology of Women Quarterly, 22*, 177–195.

Pence, E., & Paymar, M. (1993). *Education groups for men who batter: The Duluth model.* New York: Springer.

Pickett, R. (2004). *Sideways.* New York: St. Martin's Griffin.

Potter-Efron, R., & Potter-Efron, P. (2006). *Letting go of anger: The eleven most common anger styles and what to do about them.* Oakland, CA: New Harbinger.

Prochaska, J. O., & DiClemente, C. C. (1984). *The transtheoretical approach: Crossing the traditional boundaries of therapy.* Homewood, IL: Dow Jones-Irwin.

Real, T., & Johnson, S. (2012). Confrontation in couples therapy—Who needs it? *Psychotherapy Networker, 36*(2), 46–61.

Schecter, S., & Ganley, A. L. (1995). *Domestic violence: A national curriculum for family preservation practitioners.* San Francisco: Family Violence Prevention Fund.

Schiraldi, G. R. (2001). *The self-esteem workbook.* Oakland, CA: New Harbinger.

Shorey, R. C., Febres, J., Brasfield, H., & Stuart, G. L. (2011). *A descriptive investigation of proximal factors to female perpetrated psychological aggression in dating relationships. Partner Abuse, 2*(2), 131–146.

Sielski, C., Begun, A., & Hamel, J. (2015). Expanding knowledge concerning the Safe at Home instruments for assessing readiness-to-change among individuals in batterer treatment. *Partner Abuse, 6*(3), 255–272.

Simmons, C. A., Lehmann, P., Cobb, N., & Fowler, C. R. (2005). Personality profiles of women and men arrested for domestic violence: An analysis of similarities and differences. *Journal of Offender Rehabilitation, 41*(4), 63–81.

Sorenson, S. B., Upchurch, D. M., & Shen, H. (1996). Violence and injury in marital arguments: Risk patterns and gender differences. *American Journal of Public Health, 86*, 35–40.

Stark, E. (2006). Commentary on Johnson's "Conflict and Control: Gender Symmetry and Asymmetry in Domestic Violence." *Violence Against Women, 12*(11), 1019–1025. doi:10.1177/1077801206293329

Stets, J. E., & Straus, M. A. (1990). Gender differences in reporting marital violence and its medical and psychological consequences. In M. A. Straus & R. J. Gelles (Eds.), *Physical violence in American families: Risk factors and adaptations to violence in 8,145 families* (pp. 227–244). New Brunswick, NJ: Transaction.

Stuart, G. L., Moore, T. M., Gordon, K. C., Hellmuth, J. C., Ramsey, S. E., & Kahler, C. W. (2006). Reasons for intimate partner violence perpetration among arrested women. *Violence Against Women, 12*, 609–621.

Straus, M. A. (1999). The controversy over domestic violence by women: A methodological, theoretical, and sociology of science analysis. In X. B. Arriaga & S. Oskamp (Eds.), *Violence in intimate relationships* (pp. 17–44). Thousand Oaks, CA: Sage.

Straus, M. A., Hamby, S. L., Boney-McCoy, S. U. E., & Sugarman, D. B. (1996). The revised Conflict Tactics Scales (CTS2): Development and preliminary psychometric data. *Journal of Family Issues, 17* (3), 283–316. https://doi.org/10.1177/019251396017003001

Straus, M. A., & Sweet, S. (1992). Verbal/symbolic aggression in couples: Incidence rates and relationships to personal characteristics. *Journal of Marriage and Family, 54*(2), 346–357.

Struckman-Johnson, C., Struckman-Johnson, D., & Anderson, P. B. (2003). Tactics of sexual coercion: When men and women won't take no for an answer. *Journal of Sex Research, 40*(1), 76–86.

Stuart, G. L., Moore, M. T., Gordon, K. C., Hellmuth, J. C., Ramsey, S. E., & Kahler, C. W. (2006). Reasons for intimate partner violence perpetration among arrested women. *Violence Against Women, 12*, 609–621. https://doi.org/10.1177/1077801206290173

Swan, S. C. (2005, August 10). *A review of research on women's use of violence with male intimate partners, and a typology of women who use violence* [Paper presentation]. Department of Defense Domestic Violence Intervention/Treatment Protocol Development Working Meeting, Alexandria, VA.

Swan, S. C., Gambone, L., & Fields, A. (2004). Technical report for "An empirical examination of a theory of women's use of violence in intimate relationships." Washington, DC: National Institute of Justice.

Swan, S. C., & Snow, D. L. (2002). A typology of women's use of violence in intimate relationships. *Violence Against Women, 8*(3), 286–319.

Swan, S. C., & Snow, D. L. (2003). Behavioral and psychological differences among abused women who use violence in intimate relationships. *Violence Against Women, 9*(1), 75–109.

Swan, S. C., & Snow, D. L. (2006). The development of a theory of women's use of violence in intimate relationships. *Violence Against Women, 12.*

Tjaden, P. T., & Thoennes, N. (2000). *Extent, nature, and consequences of intimate partner violence: Findings from the National Violence Against Women Survey.* Washington, DC: National Institute of Justice.

Varley Thornton, A. J., Graham-Kevan, N., & Archer, J. (2010). Adaptive and maladaptive personality traits as predictors of violent and nonviolent offending behavior in men and women. *Aggressive Behavior, 36*, 177–186.

Vivian, D., & Langhinrichsen-Rohling, J. (1994). Are bi-directionally violent couples mutually victimized? A gender-sensitve comparison. *Violence and Victims, 9*(2), 107–124.

Wachtel, E. (2019, March/April). Storm damage. *Psychotherapy Networker*, 61–64.

Walker, L. (2009). *The battered woman syndrome* (3rd ed.). New York: Springer.

Weizmann-Henelius, G., Matti Grönroos, L., Putkonen, H., Eronen, M., Lindberg, N., & Häkkänen-Nyholm, H. (2011). Gender-specific risk factors for intimate partner homicide: a nationwide register-based study. *Journal of Interpersonal Violence, 27*(8), 1519–1539. doi: 10.1177/0886260511425793

West, C. M., & Rose, S. (2000). Dating aggression among low income African American youth: An examination of gender differences and antagonistic beliefs. *Violence Against Women, 6*, 470–495.

Weston, R., Marshall, L. L., & Coker, A. L. (2007). Women's motives for violent and nonviolent behaviors in conflicts. *Journal of Interpersonal Violence, 22*(8), 1043–1065.

Wexler, D. B. (1991). *The adolescent self: Strategies for self-management, self-soothing, and selfesteem in adolescence.* New York: Norton.

Wexler, D. (2016). *The STOP program for women who abuse.* New York: Norton.

Wexler, D. B. (2020). *The STOP domestic violence program* (4th ed., rev. and updated). New York: Norton.

Whitfield, C. L., Anda, R. F., Dube, S. R., & Felitti, V. J. (2003). Violent childhood experiences and the risk of intimate partner violence in adults: Assessment in a large health maintenance organization. *Journal of Interpersonal Violence, 18*(2), 166–185. doi:https://doi.org/10.1177/0886260502238733

Yalom, I. (1995). *The theory and practice of group psychotherapy* (3rd ed.). New York: Basic Books.

Yllo, K. A. (1993). Through a feminist lens: Gender, power and violence. In R. J. Gelles & D. R. Loseke (Eds.), *Current controversies on family violence* (pp. 47–62). Newbury Park, CA: Sage.

Yourstone, J., Lindholm, T., & Kristiansson, M. (2008). Women who kill: A comparison of the psychosocial background of female and male perpetrators. *International Journal of Law and Psychiatry, 31*(4), 374–383. doi:10.1016/j.ijlp.2008.06.005

Index

Note: Italicized page locators refer to figures.

About the Author

David B. Wexler, PhD, is a clinical psychologist in private practice in San Diego, specializing in the treatment of relationships in conflict. He is the executive director of the nonprofit Relationship Training Institute (RTI), which provides education and treatment internationally for relationship development and the prevention and treatment of relationship violence. He has also served as the clinical and administrative supervisor for the NIMH-sponsored research study of domestic violence in the Navy.

Dr. Wexler is the author of several books, including *When Good Men Behave Badly: Change Your Behavior, Change Your Relationship* (2004), and *#MeToo-Informed Therapy: Counseling Approaches for Men, Women, and Couples* (with Holly B. Sweet, 2021). He has been featured on the *Dr. Phil* show and the *TODAY* show, in the *Wall Street Journal*, *Washington Post*, "*O*" magazine, *Cosmopolitan*, *Redbook*, *Men's Health*, and on hundreds of radio and TV programs throughout North America to help educate the public about relationships in conflict and how to resolve them.

Additionally, Dr. Wexler has authored an internationally-recognized domestic violence treatment manual: the newly revised and updated *The STOP Program: Fourth Edition*, and has trained thousands of community professionals, military personnel, and law enforcement officials through extensive training seminars on *The STOP Program* model throughout the world.

To contact Dr. Wexler or other RTI faculty about professional training or consultation, please go to the RTI website at www.RTIprojects.org or contact him directly at dbwexler@gmail.com.